TOEIC®テスト これだけ 直前1カ月 350点クリア

How to Prepare for the TOEIC® Test : Introductory Course

鹿野晴夫

研究社

Copyright © 2011 by ICC
『TOEIC®テスト　これだけ　直前1カ月　350点クリア』

PRINTED IN JAPAN

はじめに

●本書を手にされたみなさんへ

　本書『TOEIC®テスト　これだけ　直前1カ月　350点クリア』を手に取っていただき、誠にありがとうございます。
ところで、みなさんが本書を手にされた理由は何でしょうか？　その理由が下記のものであれば、まさに本書はお探しの本です。

① 英語が超苦手、または現在のTOEICスコアが350点未満
② TOEICテスト受験までの1カ月間で、成果を出したい
③ 通勤・通学など、移動時間を有効に使いたい

　TOEICテストに受験申し込みをしたあと、試験までの1カ月間に何をするか？　これがポイントです。多くの方は、TOEICテストの問題集で学習を始めます。確かにTOEICテストは、Part 1〜Part 7に分かれていて、問題形式がそれぞれ異なりますから、それに慣れていないと、高いスコアは望めません。
　ですので、テスト前に問題形式に慣れておくことは絶対に必要です。でも、試験までの1カ月間、ただ漠然と問題集を解くだけでは、実力アップは望めません。問題を解くだけでなく、復習が必要なのです。
　しかし、1カ月間でどれほどの復習ができるでしょうか？
　1日平均3時間、月100時間以上学習できる方は別として、満足に復習できないまま、試験当日を迎えてしまう方も少なくないでしょう。本書『TOEIC®テスト　これだけ　直前1カ月　350点クリア』は、通勤・通学の時間くらいしか使えない方も、問題形式に慣れるだけでなく、実力アップがはかれるように、工夫しました。本書には、次の特長があります。

① **300点台から出発した著者のノウハウを凝縮**
　私のTOEICテスト初受験は、社会人29歳の時、スコアは335点でした。まさに、「350点クリア」が最初の目標だったのです。そこから、1年で610点、2年3カ月で760点、3年半で850点になりました。900点突破には、7年かかりましたが、初受験からのスコアアップは、600点以上です。
　TOEICスコアは、350点・470点・600点と、壁を超えるように伸びていきます。「350点の壁」は、誰にでも超えられそうですが、そうでもありません。事実、企業・学校内で実施されているTOEIC IPテストの結果では、340点以下の方が30％を占めています。
　なぜ350点をクリアできない方が多いのでしょう？　それは、「どうやって学習したらいいかわからない」という人が多いからです。本書は、英語が超苦手な方も、迷わず1カ月間トレーニングできるように、工夫しています。

② **1カ月間で、問題形式に慣れるだけでなく、実力アップ**
　TOEICテストが測る英語力は、「スピード対応能力」です。具体的には、「速い英語が聴ける」「意味の通じる語句をすぐに選べる」「速く読める」ということです。本書は、みなさんがTOEICの問題形式に慣れつつ、このスピード対応能力も同時にアップできるように計算のうえ、編纂しました。

③ **テキストで学習し、音声CDで復習できる**
　クイズ形式で練習問題を解き、解答・解説を確認したあと、音声CDを利用して、通学・通勤などのあいだに効果的に学習できるように工夫しました。
　みなさんが、本書を上手に活用し、TOEICテスト受験までの1カ月間の学習を効果的に進めていただけることを願っています。

2011年3月

鹿野　晴夫

『TOEIC® テスト　これだけ　直前1カ月　350点クリア』
目次

はじめに ……………………………………………… 3

第1章　直前1カ月でも差がつくトレーニング法 ……… 7

第2章　Week 1 ……………………………………… 13

第3章　Week 2 ……………………………………… 49

第4章　Week 3 ……………………………………… 85

第5章　Week 4 ……………………………………… 121

第6章　最終チェック ……………………………… 157

効果的に学習できるように、各レッスンの CD トラック番号は前から振っていないのでご注意ください（12 ページをご覧ください）。
　各レッスンの最初のトラックで Week 1 Day 1, Week 1 Day 2, Week 1 Day 3...とナレーションが入りますが、このトラック番号は記してありません。

第 **1** 章

直前1カ月でも差がつくトレーニング法

1. 学習の進め方

❶ 350点クリアに必要な力を理解する

　まず、TOEICテストで350点をクリアする正答目標を確認しましょう。正答目標には、偶然に正解するものを含みます。TOEICテストは、Part 2が3択、他のパートは4択ですから、ただ勘で解答用紙にマークしても、Part 2は33％、他のパートは25％の確率で正答します。

　出題数が多く、正答目標の高いパートは、Part 2、Part 5、Part 7のシングルパッセージです。3つの合計は98問で、そのうち49問が正答目標です。ですから、TOEICテスト受験まで1カ月を切ったら、迷わずこの3つのパートのスコアアップをめざして、トレーニングを行ないましょう。

　一方、出題数の多くないパート（Part 1、Part 6）、正答目標の高くないパート（Part 3、Part 4、Part 7のダブルパッセージ）については、問題形式に慣れることをまず考えましょう。

350点クリアのための正答目標

セクション	Part	形式	問題数	正答目標
リスニング 100問 （45分間）	1	写真描写問題	10問	60％
	2	応答問題	30問	50％
	3	会話問題	30問	30％
	4	説明文問題	30問	30％
リーディング 100問 （75分間）	5	短文穴埋め問題	40問	50％
	6	長文穴埋め問題	12問	45％
	7	読解問題（シングルパッセージ）	28問	50％
		読解問題（ダブルパッセージ）	20問	30％

❷ 1カ月間の学習の流れ

　本書を活用した TOEIC テスト受験前1カ月間の学習の流れは、以下のとおりです。第2章～第5章の4章を1週間に1章のペースで進めて、受験直前に第6章を学習して、最終チェックをします。また、本書付属の CD を通勤・通学などのあいだに聞くことで、復習も効果的にできます。

章	週	テキスト学習内容	音声CD
第2章	Week 1	Day 1 会話文トレーニング	移動時間を活用して音声CDで復習
		Day 2 会話文トレーニング	
		Day 3 会話文トレーニング	
		Day 4 会話文トレーニング	
		Day 5 説明文トレーニング	
		Day 6 チェックテスト	
第3章	Week 2	Week 1 同様	
第4章	Week 3		
第5章	Week 4		
第6章	受験直前	問題形式の最終チェック	

❸ 会話文・説明文トレーニングの英文

　会話文トレーニングの英文は、Part 2（応答問題）の形式に近い問題を3問組み合わせました。Part 2 は、話し手 A の短い問いかけに、話し手 B が発する4つの回答から最適なものを選ぶ問題です。本番の TOEIC では1問ずつすべて状況が異なりますが、これだと場面や状況といった周辺情報がなく、記憶に残りません。そこで本書では同じ状況を背景にした問題を3問組み合わせて、効果的にトレーニングできるようにしました。

　説明文トレーニングの英文は、Part 7（読解問題）の形式に近い英文です。会話文・説明文ともに、TOEIC テストで出題される日常生活とビジネスに関する話題を扱っています。リスニング・リーディング・文法・語彙を同じ英文でトレーニングすることで、音と文字の両面からスピード対応能力が強化でき、文法・語彙も自然と身に付きます。

2. トレーニングの方法

❶ 会話文・説明文トレーニングのステップ

　本書でメインとなる第 2 章〜第 4 章の Day 1〜 Day 5 のトレーニングです。トレーニングは、以下の Step 1〜6 の順で、1 回のトレーニング時間は約 20〜40 分です。

Step	内容	目的	時間
1	リスニング問題 (Part 3, 4 形式 3 問)	Part 3, 4 の問題形式に慣れ、 Part 2 の正答数アップをめざす。	2 分
2	リーディング問題 (Part 7 形式 3 問)	Part 7 の問題形式に慣れ、 Part 7 の正答数アップをめざす。	3 分
3	文法・語彙問題 (Part 5 形式 5 問)	Part 5 の問題形式に慣れ、 Part 5 の正答数アップをめざす。	2 分
4	解答・解説チェック	解答・解説をチェックし、現時点での理解度を確認する。	3 分
5	直読直解トレーニング	直読直解トレーニングで、リスニング・リーディング力を伸ばす。	5〜15 分
6	基本構文トレーニング	基本構文トレーニングで、文法・語彙力を伸ばす。	5〜15 分

❷ 直読直解トレーニングの方法 ＜基本編＞

　TOEIC テストでは、ナチュラルスピード（1 分間に 150 語以上）の英文を聞き、リーディング問題を最後まで解くには 1 分間に 150 語以上読まなければなりません。速読速聴が、まず求められます。1 分間に 150 語以上「聞いて・読む」ことができれば、TOEIC 600 点以上のスコアが期待できます。ですから、350 点クリアをめざす段階では、1 分間に 100 語以上、聞けて、読めることを

目標にしましょう。そのためには、うしろから訳して考えることなく、英語の語順どおりに理解しましょう。その練習が、「直読直解トレーニング」です。

　直読直解トレーニングの英文は、意味の区切りにスラッシュ（／）が入れてあり、意味の区切りごとに日本語訳を付けました。この英文を使って、区切り単位で、意味を理解する練習を行ないます。

直読直解トレーニング	1	CD（英語）を聞いて、英文を目で追う。
	2	CD（英語）を聞いて、日本語訳を目で追う。
	3	カンマ（,）、ピリオド（.）、スラッシュ（/）の単位で、英文の意味が理解できるか確認（理解できない部分は、日本語訳や語彙を参照）。

❸ 基本構文トレーニングの方法 ＜基本編＞

　TOEICテストには、空欄補充問題（Part 5, 6）もあります。文法・語彙問題ですが、30秒で解かないと、読解問題（Part 7）をやり残してしまいます。これは、「話す力」や「書く力」に通じるスピード対応能力を測る問題です。この能力を養うために、練習問題を解いたあと、問われていた文法・語彙を含んだ英文（基本構文）を使って、「基本構文トレーニング」を行ないます。

　われわれが母国語（日本語）を文法や語彙の理屈を意識しないで使えるのはどうしてでしょう？　それは、「リクツ」を考えなくても使えてしまう「リズム」を身に付けているからです。このリズムを身に付けるには、音読がいちばん。小学校の頃、毎日音読したのと一緒です。なお、電車の中などでは、小声か実際に声を出さない「口パク」でも効果があります。

基本構文トレーニング	1	1文ずつCD（日本語・英語）を聞き、英語を数回音読。
	2	10文の英語を続けて音読（数回）。
	3	テキストを縦に半分に折り、英語部分を見て意味がすぐにわかるか確認。

❹ チェックテスト

　第2章〜第4章のDay 6では、「チェックテスト」を行ないます。ここで、

Day 1〜Day 5で登場した単語50個の意味を確認します。Day 1〜Day 5のトレーニングの段階で、出てきた単語を意識して覚える必要はありません。Day 6のチェックテストで間違った単語の意味を確認し、通勤、通学の時間などを使って付属のCDでその音を聞けば、自然とインプットされるはずです。

5 第6章「最終チェック」

TOEICテストの問題形式を確認する25問の練習問題（約15分）です。第2章〜第5章のトレーニングを終えて、TOEICテスト受験直前に、問題形式の最終確認をして、本番に備えてください。

6 付属CDの活用方法

付属の音声CDは、下記のように構成されています。意識せずに、聞き流すだけで、語彙・基本構文の復習ができます。繰り返し聞きましょう。

CD音声が流れる順	収録	例
1	語句（日→英）	正気でない→ crazy
2	基本構文（日→英）	人は、運転中に信じられないことをします。People do some crazy things while driving.
3	本文（英）	People do some crazy things while driving : applying makeup, watching TV,
	設問（英）	1. Who is the speaker talking to?

（※効果的に学習できるように、各レッスンのCDトラック番号は前から順に振っていません。ご注意ください。）

何度も聞いて英文になじんできたら、発音された単語を続いて言ってみる（crazyのあとで、crazyと発音する）、基本構文の日本語を聞いたあと、英語の部分でシャドウイングしてみたり（少し遅れて、声をかぶせるようにつぶやく）、設問のあとでテキストを見ずに答えを考えるなどすれば、さらに効果的です。

第 **2** 章

Week 1

Week 1
今週のトレーニング

Day 1〜 Day 5 のトレーニング

Step	内容		時間
1	リスニング問題（3問）		2分
2	リーディング問題（3問）		3分
3	文法・語彙問題（5問）		2分
4	解答・解説チェック		3分
5	直読直解トレーニング		5〜15分
	①	CD（英語）を聞いて、英文を目で追う。	
	②	CD（英語）を聞いて、日本語訳を目で追う。	
	③	カンマ (,)、ピリオド (.)、スラッシュ (/) の単位で、英文の意味が理解できるか確認（理解できない部分は、日本語訳や語彙を参照）。	
6	基本構文トレーニング		5〜15分
	①	1文ずつCD（日本語・英語）を聞き、英語を数回音読。	
	②	10文の英語を続けて音読（数回行なう）。	
	③	テキストを縦に半分に折るなどして日本語訳を隠し、英語部分を見て意味がすぐにわかるか確認。	

<ワンポイント>

　まず、上記の基本的な手順に沿って、トレーニングしてください。Step 1「リスニング問題」がむずかしく感じられるかもしれません。これは、TOEIC Part 3, 4 形式の問題ですから、むずかしく感じて当然です。8ページで説明したように、Part 3, 4 は形式に慣れておくことが目的です。「まだできなくて当然」くらいの気持ちで挑戦してみてください。問題が解けなくても、落ち込む必要はありません。手順に沿ってトレーニングすれば、確実に実力はアップします。今日より、明日はもっとできるようになっている、と信じて、前向きに取り組みましょう。

Week 1

 Day 1 会話文トレーニング

Step 1 リスニング問題
CDを聞いて、問題を解こう。＜制限時間2分＞

Q1. Who is the woman?
　　(A) A flight attendant
　　(B) A baggage handler
　　(C) A traveler
　　(D) A pilot

Q2. What is the woman going to do in San Antonio?
　　(A) See a relative
　　(B) Visit her grandfather
　　(C) Change planes
　　(D) Start a new job

Q3. At the end of the conversation, what did the woman ask about?
　　(A) The weather
　　(B) Her ticket
　　(C) Her bags
　　(D) The parking lot

Step 2 リーディング問題

英文を読んで、問題を解こう。＜制限時間3分＞

M:　Where are you headed for today, ma'am?
W:　San Antonio. I'm going to see my grandmother.

M:　Do you have any bags to check?
W:　Just this one. I can carry on these two, can't I?
M:　No, just one carry-on and your shoulder bag are allowed. I'm afraid you'll have to check one of those other small bags.

M:　There you go. You're all set. I've got you in an aisle seat on both flights. Your flight to San Antonio via Denver leaves from Gate B15. Boarding begins at 12:25.
W:　And my bags are checked straight through to Antonio, correct?

Q4.　How many bags will the woman have to check in?
　　　(A) None　　　　　　　　(B) One
　　　(C) Two　　　　　　　　 (D) Three

Q5.　What is true of the woman's trip?
　　　(A) She will fly nonstop to San Antonio.
　　　(B) She will make one stop before San Antonio.
　　　(C) She will make two stops before San Antonio.
　　　(D) She will fly first to San Antonio, then to Denver.

Q6.　Why is 12:25 mentioned?
　　　(A) The plane will land at that time.
　　　(B) The plane will leave at that time.
　　　(C) Passengers will reach San Antonio at that time.
　　　(D) Passengers can start getting on the plane at that time.

Step 3　文法・語彙問題

空欄にふさわしい語句を選ぼう。＜制限時間2分＞

Q7. Good morning, and where are you headed ----- today?
 (A) out
 (B) from
 (C) with
 (D) for

Q8. I'm sorry, but you'll have ----- one of those bags.
 (A) to check
 (B) checked
 (C) a check for
 (D) to be checked

Q9. You said that my bags are checked straight -----, correct?
 (A) threw
 (B) through
 (C) throw
 (D) though

Q10. Just one carry-on and your shoulder bag ----- on this flight.
 (A) allow
 (B) is allowed
 (C) are allowed
 (D) allowed

Q11. As you requested, I've got you in an aisle seat ----- flights.
 (A) both on
 (B) on both
 (C) on these both
 (D) on both of

Step 4　解答・解説チェック

現時点での理解度を確認しよう。

問題文は、搭乗前の荷物のチェックインでの会話です。

1. 正解 **(C)**。質問：「女性は、どんな人ですか？」。答え：「旅行者」。ヒント：Do you have any bags to check?
2. 正解 **(A)**。質問：「女性は、サン・アントニオで何をする予定ですか？」。答え：「親族に会う」。ヒント：I'm going to see my grandmother.
3. 正解 **(C)**。質問：「会話の最後で、女性は何について尋ねましたか？」。答え：「彼女のバッグ」。ヒント：And my bags are checked straight through to Antonio, correct?
4. 正解 **(C)**。質問：「女性は、何個のバッグをチェックインしなければなりませんか？」。答え：「2つ」。ヒント：W: Just this one. I can carry on these two, can't I?　M: No, just one carry-on and your shoulder bag are allowed. I'm afraid you'll have to check one of those other small bags.
5. 正解 **(B)**。質問：「女性の旅行に関して、正しい記述はどれですか？」。答え：「サン・アントニオに行くのに1カ所経由する」。ヒント：Your flight to San Antonio via Denver
6. 正解 **(D)**。質問：「なぜ12時25分という時刻が述べられていますか？」。答え：「その時間に乗客が搭乗を開始できる」。ヒント：Boarding begins at 12:25.
7. 正解 **(D)**。be headed for「〜に向かう」を完成させる。
8. 正解 **(A)**。have to + 動詞「〜しなければならない」を完成させる。(D) は、受動態なので文意が通じない。
9. 正解 **(B)**。be checked straight through「（荷物が）直送される」を完成させる。
10. 正解 **(C)**。「手荷物1つ、それと、ショルダーバッグが認められる」という文意から、受動態を完成させる。主語が、Just one carry-on and your shoulder bag（複数）なので、are allowed を選ぶ。
11. 正解 **(B)**。on both flights「両方の便で」を完成させる。both：両方の。

Step 5　直読直解トレーニング

速読速聴力を高めよう。

（※日本語訳は、英語の原文の順序どおりに記してあります。）

M:　Where are you headed for today, ma'am?
　　　本日は、どちらへ行かれますか、お客様？
W:　San Antonio. I'm going to see / my grandmother.
　　　サン・アントニオです。会いに行きます、祖母に。
M:　Do you have any bags / to check?
　　　バッグはありますか、お預けになる？
W:　Just this one. I can carry on these two, can't I?
　　　これだけです。こちらの2つは機内持ち込みできますよね？
M:　No, just one carry-on / and your shoulder bag are allowed.
　　　いいえ、手荷物1つ、それとショルダーバッグが認められています。
　　　I'm afraid / you'll have to check / one of those other small bags.
　　　申し訳ありませんが、お預けください、それらの小さいバッグの1つは。
M:　There you go. You're all set. I've got you in an aisle seat /
　　　はい、どうぞ。手続き終了です。通路側の席をお取りしました、
　　　on both flights. Your flight / to San Antonio via Denver /
　　　どちらの便も。お客様の便は、デンバー経由サン・アントニオ行きの、
　　　leaves from Gate B15. Boarding begins at 12:25.
　　　B15番ゲートから出発です。搭乗は12時25分に開始です。
W:　And my bags are checked straight through / to Antonio, correct?
　　　それで私のバッグは直送されますね、サン・アントニオまで？

語句		
be headed for：～に向かう		**grandmother**：祖母
carry on：～を持ち込む		**I'm afraid**：申し訳ありませんが
all set：準備ができて		**aisle**：通路
flight：飛行機の便		**via**：～経由で
leave：出発する		**boarding**：搭乗

Step 6　基本構文トレーニング

文法・語彙力を高めよう。

1	本日は、どちらへ行かれますか？	Where are you headed for today?
2	祖母に会いに行きます。	I'm going to see my grandmother.
3	お預けになるバッグはありますか？	Do you have any bags to check?
4	こちらの2つは、機内持ち込みできますよね？	I can carry on these two, can't I?
5	機内持ち込み手荷物は1つと、ショルダーバッグだけが認められています。	Just one carry-on and your shoulder bag are allowed.
6	それらのバッグのうちの1つは、お預けいただかなければなりません。	You'll have to check one of those bags.
7	はい、どうぞ。	There you go.
8	どちらの便も、通路側のお席をお取りしました。	I've got you in an aisle seat on both flights.
9	搭乗は、12時25分に開始です。	Boarding begins at 12:25.
10	私のバッグは、直送されますね？	My bags are checked straight through, correct?

Day 2　会話文トレーニング

Step 1　リスニング問題

CDを聞いて、問題を解こう。＜制限時間2分＞

Q1. Who are the people?

　(A) Computer salespeople
　(B) Coworkers
　(C) Bankers
　(D) Movers

Q2. What caused a problem for the man?

　(A) The boss
　(B) His telephone
　(C) The woman
　(D) His computer

Q3. What did the woman give the man?

　(A) Money
　(B) A computer
　(C) Advice
　(D) A phone call

Step 2　リーディング問題
英文を読んで、問題を解こう。＜制限時間3分＞

M: Ingrid, can you help me fix this? It crashes every time I double-click it.
W: No problem. Lots of people at the office are having that problem. It's just a small conflict with something in your extensions folder.

M: It seems to be working well now. Thanks a million.
W: If you have any more trouble, the best bet is just to reinstall the software.
M: Do you have the disc for that? I think I lost mine when we moved.

M: Anyway, I can call you, if need be. You're Extension 14, right?
W: That's right, Extension 14. Take it easy, Casey.

Q4. What is true of the man and woman?
　　(A) They are having a conflict.
　　(B) Their desks are side by side.
　　(C) They work in the same office.
　　(D) Their friend is a computer expert.

Q5. What has the man lost?
　　(A) His job
　　(B) A software disc
　　(C) Some files on his computer
　　(D) The woman's telephone number

Q6. What does the woman say about the man's problem?
　　(A) It is easy to fix.
　　(B) It is very serious.
　　(C) She has had the same problem.
　　(D) She does not know how to fix it.

Step 3　文法・語彙問題
空欄にふさわしい語句を選ぼう。＜制限時間2分＞

Q7. It seems ----- well now, but let me know if you have any more trouble.
　　(A) to be worked
　　(B) be working
　　(C) to be working
　　(D) worked

Q8. When that happens, the best ----- is just to reinstall the software.
　　(A) bet
　　(B) disc
　　(C) program
　　(D) act

Q9. I can call you if need -----, but I think everything is OK now.
　　(A) be
　　(B) to
　　(C) it
　　(D) you

Q10. Something is wrong with the program, because it crashes ----- I double-click it.
　　(A) all time　　　　(B) all times
　　(C) every time　　(D) some time

Q11. It's just a small conflict with -----, but it's not a serious problem.
　　(A) anything
　　(B) something
　　(C) nothing
　　(D) a thing

Step 4　解答・解説チェック

現時点での理解度を確認しよう。

問題文は、パソコンの具合が悪くて困っている男性と、それを直す女性の会話です。

1. 正解 **(B)**。質問：「話し手たちは、どんな人ですか？」。答え：「同僚」。ヒント：Lots of people at the office are having that problem., You're Extension 14, right? など。
2. 正解 **(D)**。質問：「男性の問題の原因は、何ですか？」。答え：「彼のコンピュータ」。ヒント：can you help me fix this? It crashes every time I double-click it.
3. 正解 **(C)**。質問：「女性は、男性に何を与えましたか？」。答え：「助言」。ヒント：If you have any more trouble, the best bet is just to reinstall the software.
4. 正解 **(C)**。質問：「男性と女性について、正しい記述はどれですか？」。答え：「彼らは、同じ職場で働いている」。ヒント：Q1同様。
5. 正解 **(B)**。質問：「男性は、何をなくしましたか？」。答え：「ソフトウエアのディスク」。ヒント：I think I lost mine when we moved.
6. 正解 **(A)**。質問：「女性は、男性の問題について何と言っていますか？」。答え：「修理は容易」。ヒント：No problem.
7. 正解 **(C)**。seem to be ＋動詞ing「～しているように思われる」を完成させる。(A)は受動態「動かされる」で、文意が通じない。
8. 正解 **(A)**。the best bet「最良の策」を完成させる。
9. 正解 **(A)**。if need be「必要なら」を完成させる。
10. 正解 **(C)**。every time ＋節「～するたびに」を完成させる。
11. 正解 **(B)**。「何かとのコンフリクト」が問題になっているので、something「特定できない何か」を選ぶ。

Step 5　直読直解トレーニング

速読速聴力を高めよう。

（※日本語訳は、英語の原文の順序どおりに記してあります。）

M: Ingrid, can you help me / fix this?
　　イングリッド、手伝ってくれますか、これを直すのを？
　　It crashes / every time I double-click it.
　　クラッシュします、ダブルクリックするたびに。

W: No problem. Lots of people at the office are / having that problem.
　　まかせてください。オフィスのたくさんの人びとが、その問題を抱えています。
　　It's just a small conflict / with something / in your extensions folder.
　　それは、ちょっとしたコンフリクトです、何かとの、拡張フォルダー内の。

M: It seems / to be working well now. Thanks a million.
　　～のようです、今は順調に動いている。本当にありがとうございます。

W: If you have any more trouble, the best bet is /
　　もし、まだ何か問題が起きたら、最良の策は、
　　just to reinstall the software.
　　ソフトを再インストールすることです。

M: Do you have the disc for that?
　　それ用のディスクを持っていますか？
　　I think / I lost mine / when we moved.
　　思います、なくしたと、引っ越した時に。

M: Anyway, I can call you, if need be. You're Extension 14, right?
　　とにかく、電話していいですね、必要な時は。あなたは、内線14ですね？

W: That's right, Extension 14. Take it easy, Casey.
　　そうです、内線14です。じゃあね、ケーシー。

語句
crash：プログラムが動かなくなる　　conflict：衝突　　work：作動する
trouble：困難　　bet：取るべき策　　reinstall：～を再インストールする
disc：ディスク　　move：引っ越しする　　anyway：とにかく　　extension：内線

Step 6 基本構文トレーニング
文法・語彙力を高めよう。

11	これを直すのを手伝ってくれますか？	Can you help me fix this?
12	ダブルクリックするたびにクラッシュします。	It crashes every time I double-click it.
13	オフィスのたくさんの人びとが、その問題を抱えています。	Lots of people at the office are having that problem.
14	それは、何かとのちょっとしたコンフリクトにすぎません。	It's just a small conflict with something.
15	今は、順調に動いているようです。	It seems to be working well now.
16	本当にありがとうございます。	Thanks a million.
17	最良の策は、ソフトを再インストールすることです。	The best bet is just to reinstall the software.
18	それ用のディスクを持っていますか？	Do you have the disc for that?
19	引っ越した時に、自分のをなくしたと思います。	I think I lost mine when we moved.
20	あなたに電話してもいいですよね、必要な時は。	I can call you, if need be.

Week 1

Day 3 会話文トレーニング

Step 1 リスニング問題
CDを聞いて、問題を解こう。＜制限時間2分＞

Q1. Who are the people?
  (A) A teacher and a student
  (B) A husband and wife
  (C) A doctor and a patient
  (D) A clerk and a customer

Q2. What did the woman forget to bring?
  (A) Her Club Card number
  (B) Her Club Card
  (C) Her coupon
  (D) Her purse

Q3. What is clear from the conversation?
  (A) How much the woman spent
  (B) What the woman bought
  (C) Where the woman lives
  (D) How old the woman is

Step 2 リーディング問題

英文を読んで、問題を解こう。＜制限時間3分＞

M: Hi, there. How are you doing today? Do you have a Club Card?
W: I'm fine. Sorry, I forgot my card, but I remember my number. It's 404-8891.

M: Ma'am, I'm sorry, but that coupon is not good anymore. It expired at the end of last month.
W: Oh, well. Just ring it up anyway. How much is the regular price, by the way?
M: If you add one more, they're on special at five for $5.00.

M: Four for $3.33...$1.79...$9.50...and your total comes to $34.56.
W: OK, put it on my card, please.

Q4. What does the woman bring with her?
　(A) A coupon
　(B) Her Club Card
　(C) A telephone number
　(D) Her Club Card and a coupon

Q5. What does the man suggest that the woman do?
　(A) Get a new Club Card.
　(B) Buy five items for $5.00.
　(C) Ask for a new discount coupon.
　(D) Pay the regular price and get a coupon later.

Q6. What is the total number of items bought by the woman?
　(A) Five　　　　　　(B) Eight
　(C) Eleven　　　　　(D) The information is not in the passage.

Step 3　文法・語彙問題

空欄にふさわしい語句を選ぼう。＜制限時間2分＞

Q7.　I don't care how much it costs; just ring ------ anyway.
　　　(A) it up
　　　(B) up it
　　　(C) it
　　　(D) up

Q8.　They're ------ at five for $5.00, which is a big bargain.
　　　(A) especially
　　　(B) special
　　　(C) especially on
　　　(D) on special

Q9.　With everything included, your total ------ to $34.56.
　　　(A) reaches
　　　(B) adds
　　　(C) arrives
　　　(D) comes

Q10. I'm sorry, but that coupon is not good -----.
　　　(A) some more
　　　(B) anymore
　　　(C) no longer
　　　(D) until now

Q11. I don't have much cash with me, so put it ----- my card, please.
　　　(A) out
　　　(B) in
　　　(C) on
　　　(D) off

Step 4　解答・解説チェック

現時点での理解度を確認しよう。

問題文は、スーパーのレジでのやり取りです。

1. 正解 **(D)**。質問：「話し手たちは、どんな人ですか？」。答え：「店員と客」。ヒント：Just ring it up anyway, put it on my card, please など。
2. 正解 **(B)**。質問：「女性は、何を持ってくるのを忘れましたか？」。答え：「彼女のクラブカード」。ヒント：Sorry, I forgot my card.
3. 正解 **(A)**。質問：「この会話で明らかなことは、何ですか？」。答え：「女性が使った金額」。ヒント：your total comes to $34.56.
4. 正解 **(A)**。質問：「女性は何を持っていますか？」。答え：「クーポン券」。ヒント：that coupon is not good anymore
5. 正解 **(B)**。質問：「男性は、女性に何をするよう提案しますか？」。答え：「5つで5ドルの商品を買うこと」。ヒント：If you add one more, they're on special at five for $5.00.
6. 正解 **(D)**。質問：「女性が購入した商品は、全部でいくつですか？」。答え：「その情報は述べられていない」。ヒント：合計数は述べられていない。
7. 正解 **(A)**。ring up「〜をレジに打つ」を完成させる。目的語（「〜をレジに打つ」の、〜の部分）が代名詞（it など）の場合は、ring it up の語順になるので (B) (D) は、不可。
8. 正解 **(D)**。on special「特別価格で」を完成させる。
9. 正解 **(D)**。come to「（合計が）〜になる」の3人称単数現在形を完成させる。
10. 正解 **(B)**。否定文で「もはや〜でない」を意味する anymore を選ぶ。(A)「（さらに）もう少し」。(C) も「もはや〜でない」だが、that coupon is no longer good の形になる。
11. 正解 **(C)**。put 〜 on one's card「〜をカードで支払う」を完成させる。

Step 5　直読直解トレーニング

速読速聴力を高めよう。

(※日本語訳は、英語の原文の順序どおりに記しています。)

M: Hi, there. How are you doing today? Do you have a Club Card?
　　こんにちは。今日は、ご機嫌いかが？　クラブカードをお持ちですか？
W: I'm fine. Sorry, I forgot my card, but I remember my number.
　　元気です。すみません、カードを忘れました、でも番号は覚えています。
　　It's 404-8891.
　　404-8891 です。

M: Ma'am, I'm sorry, but that coupon is not good anymore.
　　お客様、申し訳ありません、そのクーポンはもうご利用になれません。
　　It expired / at the end of last month.
　　それは期限切れになりました、先月末で。
W: Oh, well. Just ring it up / anyway.
　　あら、まあ。レジを打ってください、いずれにしても。
　　How much / is the regular price, by the way?
　　おいくらですか、通常価格では、ところで？
M: If you add one more, they're on special / at five for $5.00.
　　もう1つ追加なされば、特価になります、5つで5ドルの。

M: Four for $3.33.../ $1.79.../ $9.50... /
　　4つで3ドル33セント、1ドル79セント、9ドル50セント、
　　and your total comes to $34.56.
　　それで合計は34ドル56セントになります。
W: OK, put it on my card, please.
　　わかりました、カードでお願いします。

語句　**Hi, there.**：こんにちは。　**forget**：〜を忘れる　**good**：有効　**expire**：期限が切れる
　　ring up：(〜を)レジに打つ　**anyway**：とにかく　**by the way**：ところで
　　add：〜を加える　**on special**：特別価格で　**come to**：(金額が)〜になる

Step 6 基本構文トレーニング

文法・語彙力を高めよう。

21	今日は、ご機嫌いかがですか？	How are you doing today?
22	クラブカードは、お持ちですか？	Do you have a Club Card?
23	カードを忘れてきました。	I forgot my card.
24	そのクーポンはもうご利用になれません。	That coupon is not good anymore.
25	先月末で期限切れになりました。	It expired at the end of last month.
26	とにかく、レジを打ってください。	Just ring it up anyway.
27	通常価格はいくらですか？	How much is the regular price?
28	それらは、5つで5ドルの特価です。	They're on special at five for $5.00.
29	合計で34ドル56セントになります。	Your total comes to $34.56.
30	クレジットカードでお願いします。	Put it on my card, please.

Week 1

Day 4 会話文トレーニング

Step 1 リスニング問題
CDを聞いて、問題を解こう。＜制限時間2分＞

Q1. When did the conversation take place?
　　(A) During breakfast
　　(B) Around noon
　　(C) In the afternoon
　　(D) At night

Q2. Where did the man go?
　　(A) Outside
　　(B) To the roof of the house
　　(C) Downstairs
　　(D) To a neighbor's house

Q3. What did the man find?
　　(A) An animal
　　(B) A burglar
　　(C) A policeman
　　(D) A baby

Step 2　リーディング問題

英文を読んで、問題を解こう。＜制限時間 3 分＞

W:　Jason! Jason! Wake up! I heard a noise downstairs.
M:　Huh? What? Oh, it's probably nothing. Go back to sleep.

W:　Now do you believe me? I'm calling 911.
M:　Hold on. Let me go check it out first before we start calling the cops.
W:　What if it's a burglar, or worse?! Just be careful. Here, take that baseball bat.

W:　Jason! Jason? Who's down there? A cat? Aw, it's so cute.
M:　Yeah, this is our "burglar." I guess it's a stray. It must've climbed in that window there to get out of the rain.

Q4.　What was the man doing when the woman first spoke to him?
　　(A) Calling someone
　　(B) Watching a game
　　(C) Sleeping at home
　　(D) Listening to something

Q5.　Why does the man tell the woman to wait?
　　(A) First, he wants to go downstairs.
　　(B) First, he wants to call the police.
　　(C) First, he wants to find a baseball bat.
　　(D) First, he wants to see if a window is open.

Q6.　How has the weather been?
　　(A) Hot　　　　　　　　(B) Wet
　　(C) Nice　　　　　　　 (D) Cold

Step 3 文法・語彙問題

空欄にふさわしい語句を選ぼう。＜制限時間2分＞

Q7. I'm sure that I heard a ----- downstairs.
- (A) music
- (B) silence
- (C) quiet
- (D) noise

Q8. It's probably -----, so don't worry about it.
- (A) nothing
- (B) not something
- (C) no thing
- (D) none

Q9. What if it's a burglar, or -----?!
- (A) worst
- (B) bad
- (C) more badly
- (D) worse

Q10. Let me go check ----- first before you do anything.
- (A) out
- (B) out it
- (C) it
- (D) it out

Q11. It's a cat, and it must ----- in that window there.
- (A) climb
- (B) climbed
- (C) be climbing
- (D) have climbed

Step 4　解答・解説チェック

現時点での理解度を確認しよう。

問題文は、下の階で怪しい物音を聞いて不安がる男女の会話です。

1. 正解 **(D)**。質問：「この会話は、いつ行なわれましたか？」。答え：「夜に」。ヒント：Wake up!, Go back to sleep. など。
2. 正解 **(C)**。質問：「男性は、どこに行きましたか？」。答え：「階下」。ヒント：I heard a noise downstairs., Let me go check it out など。
3. 正解 **(A)**。質問：「男性は、何を見つけましたか？」。答え：「動物」。ヒント：A cat?
4. 正解 **(C)**。質問：「女性が最初に話しかけた時、男性はどうしていましたか？」。答え：「家で寝ていた」。ヒント：女性の Wake up!
5. 正解 **(A)**。質問：「男性は、なぜ女性に待つように言ったのですか？」。答え：「まず、男性が下の階に行ってみたい」。ヒント：Let me go check it out first
6. 正解 **(B)**。質問：「天候はどうでしたか？」。答え：「雨」。ヒント：It must've climbed...to get out of the rain.
7. 正解 **(D)**。文意から、noise「物音」を選ぶ。
8. 正解 **(A)**。文意から、nothing を選び、it's nothing「何でもない」を完成させる。
9. 正解 **(D)**。文意から、worse を選び、or worse「あるいはさらに悪い」を完成させる。
10. 正解 **(D)**。check out「〜を調べる」を完成させる。目的語が it（代名詞）なので、check it out の語順になる。
11. 正解 **(D)**。助動詞 must のあとの動詞は原形になるが、must climb「よじ登らなければならい」では文意が通じない。must have + 過去分詞「〜したに違いない」を完成させる。

Step 5　直読直解トレーニング
速読速聴力を高めよう。

（※日本語訳は、英語の原文の順序どおりに記してあります。）

W: Jason! Jason! Wake up! I heard a noise downstairs.
　　ジェイソン！ ジェイソン！ 起きて！ 下の階で物音がしました。
M: Huh? What? Oh, it's probably nothing. Go back to sleep.
　　え？ なに？ ああ、たぶん、なんでもありません。眠りに戻って。

W: Now do you believe me? I'm calling 911.
　　今度は、私を信じますね？ 911番に電話します。
M: Hold on. Let me go check it out first / before we start calling the cops.
　　待ってください。まず、私が行って調べます、警察に電話する前に。
W: What if / it's a burglar, or worse?!
　　どうします、強盗か、もっと悪質だったら？！
　　Just be careful. Here, take that baseball bat.
　　用心してください。ほら、あのバットを持っていってください。

W: Jason! Jason? Who's down there? A cat?
　　ジェイソン！ ジェイソン？ 下にいるのは誰？ 猫？
　　Aw, it's so cute.
　　まあ、とてもかわいい。
M: Yeah, this is our "burglar." I guess / it's a stray.
　　そうです、これがわが家の「強盗」です。思います、迷い猫だと。
　　It must've climbed in that window there / to get out of the rain.
　　よじ登って、あそこの窓から入ったに違いありません、雨を避けるために。

語句

- **noise**：物音
- **believe**：～を信じる
- **check out**：～を調べる
- **burglar**：強盗
- **cute**：かわいらしい
- **probably**：たぶん
- **Hold on**：待て
- **cops**：警察
- **careful**：注意深い
- **stray**：迷い猫

Step 6　基本構文トレーニング
文法・語彙力を高めよう。

31	下の階で物音がしました。	I heard a noise downstairs.
32	たぶん、なんでもありません。	It's probably nothing.
33	眠りに戻ってください。	Go back to sleep.
34	今度は、私を信じますね？	Now do you believe me?
35	911番に電話します。	I'm calling 911.
36	まず、私が行って調べます。	Let me go check it out first.
37	強盗か、もっと悪質だったらどうしますか？！	What if it's a burglar, or worse?!
38	ほら、あのバットを持っていってください。	Here, take that baseball bat.
39	下にいるのは誰ですか？	Who's down there?
40	よじ登って、あそこの窓から入ったに違いありません。	It must've climbed in that window there.

Day 5 説明文トレーニング

Step 1 リスニング問題
CDを聞いて、問題を解こう。＜制限時間2分＞

Q1. Before the demonstration, what did the speaker prepare?
 (A) Maps
 (B) Vegetables
 (C) Pens and pencils
 (D) Photographs

Q2. What is the speaker doing?
 (A) Washing a pan and a wok
 (B) Shopping for tofu, peas and corn
 (C) Eating a delicious meal
 (D) Showing how to fix a dish

Q3. When will the food be ready?
 (A) In 7 minutes
 (B) In 17 minutes
 (C) In 70 minutes
 (D) In about an hour

Step 2　リーディング問題
英文を読んで、問題を解こう。＜制限時間 3 分＞

OK, we have our hoisin sauce here, to which we'll add some sugar, soy sauce, and a bit of wine, and mix them together. At the same time I'm heating oil in this wok and I'll put our minced ginger and garlic in there and stir. OK, 10 seconds is enough, and we add the sauce. Stir it... one...two...three times and we add the water. Now we stir and...there it has started to bubble. In go the tofu, peas, corn, carrots, and mushrooms. Fry it a bit, and once that's done we cover the pan. Lower the heat to medium and let it simmer for seven minutes.

Q4.　How many liquids does the speaker mention?
　　(A) Two
　　(B) Three
　　(C) Four
　　(D) Five

Q5.　Which of these is NOT included in the dish?
　　(A) Meat
　　(B) Alcohol
　　(C) Vegetables
　　(D) Soy products

Q6.　How long does this dish take to prepare?
　　(A) No more than five minutes
　　(B) Less than seven minutes
　　(C) Seven minutes
　　(D) More than seven minutes

Step 3　文法・語彙問題

空欄にふさわしい語句を選ぼう。＜制限時間2分＞

Q7. We'll ---- some sugar, soy sauce, and a bit of wine.
　　(A) addition
　　(B) add
　　(C) added
　　(D) additional

Q8. ---- the tofu, peas, corn, carrots, and mushrooms.
　　(A) Go in
　　(B) In
　　(C) Go
　　(D) In go

Q9. ---- simmer for seven minutes, then it's ready to serve.
　　(A) Let it
　　(B) Let's go
　　(C) It's
　　(D) Do it

Q10. I'll put our minced ginger in there and -----.
　　(A) stirring
　　(B) to stir
　　(C) is stirred
　　(D) stir

Q11. ----- that's done we cover the pan and reduce the heat.
　　(A) One time
　　(B) On more time
　　(C) Once
　　(D) Once more

Step 4　解答・解説チェック

現時点での理解度を確認しよう。

問題文は、料理の仕方を伝える文です。

1. 正解 **(B)**。質問：「実演の前に、話し手は何を準備しましたか？」。答え：「野菜」。ヒント：In go the tofu, peas, corn, carrots, and mushrooms.
2. 正解 **(D)**。質問：「話し手は、何をしていますか？」。答え：「料理を作ってみせている」。ヒント：さまざまな食材、料理道具の名称など。
3. 正解 **(A)**。質問：「料理ができるのは、いつですか？」。答え：「7分後」。ヒント：let it simmer for seven minutes
4. 正解 **(D)**。質問：「話し手は、何種類の液体について述べていますか？」。答え：「5種類」。ヒント：hoisin sauce, soy sauce, wine, oil, water
5. 正解 **(A)**。質問：「料理に含まれていないのは、次のどれですか？」。答え：「肉」。ヒント：(B) wine (C) ginger, garlic, peas, corn, carrots, mushrooms (D) soy sauce, tofu
6. 正解 **(D)**。質問：「この料理にかかる時間は、どれくらいですか？」。答え：「7分以上」。ヒント：I'll put...and stir. (...) 10 seconds is enough, Fry it a bit, let it simmer for seven minutes など。
7. 正解 **(B)**。助動詞 will のあとなので、add「〜を加える」（動詞・原形）を選ぶ。(A)「追加」（名詞）、(D)「追加の」（形容詞）。
8. 正解 **(D)**。The tofu, peas, corn, carrots, and mushrooms go in. の倒置文（強調したい部分を前に持ってきた文）を完成させる。この場合、Go in ではなく、前置詞が前に出た In go の語順になる。
9. 正解 **(A)**。let +（人・物）+ 動詞「（人・物）に〜させる」を完成させる。
10. 正解 **(D)**。and で並列した動詞は同じ形になるので、stir（動詞・原形）を選び、I'll put 〜 and stir. を完成させる。
11. 正解 **(C)**。文意から、接続詞 once「いったん〜したら」を選ぶ。

Step 5　直読直解トレーニング

速読速聴力を高めよう。
（※日本語訳は、英語の原文の順序どおりに記してあります。）

OK, we have our hoisin sauce here, to which we'll add /
さて、ここに海鮮醤があります、これに加えます、
some sugar, soy sauce, and a bit of wine, and mix them together.
砂糖、醤油、それに少々のワインを、そして、それらを混ぜ合わせます。
At the same time / I'm heating oil / in this wok /
同時に、油を温めています、この中華鍋で、
and I'll put our minced ginger and garlic in there / and stir.
そして、みじん切りにしたショウガとニンニクをそこに入れ、かき混ぜます。
OK, 10 seconds is enough, and we add the sauce.
これでよし、10秒で十分です、そしてソースを加えます。
Stir it... / one...two...three times / and we add the water. Now we stir and... /
それをかき混ぜます、1...2...3回、そして水を加えます。次に、かき混ぜて……、
there / it has started to bubble. In go / the tofu, peas, corn, carrots,
ほら、煮立ち始めました。入ります、豆腐、エンドウ豆、コーン、ニンジン、
and mushrooms. Fry it a bit, and once that's done / we cover the pan.
それにマッシュルームが。少々炒め、それがすんだら、鍋にフタをします。
Lower the heat / to medium / and let it simmer / for seven minutes.
火を弱めます、中火に、そして煮込みます、7分間。

語句		
soy sauce：醤油		**mix**：〜を混ぜ合わせる
wok：中華鍋		**minced**：みじん切りにした
stir：〜をかき混ぜる		**bubble**：沸騰する
peas：エンドウ豆		**fry**：〜を炒める
pan：鍋		**simmer**：ことこと煮える

Step 6　基本構文トレーニング
文法・語彙力を高めよう。

41	砂糖と醤油を少々加えます。	We'll add some sugar and soy sauce.
42	この中華鍋で油を温めています。	I'm heating oil in this wok.
43	みじん切りにしたショウガをそこに入れ、かき混ぜます。	I'll put our minced ginger in there and stir.
44	10秒で十分です。	10 seconds is enough.
45	それが煮立ち始めました。	It has started to bubble.
46	豆腐、エンドウ豆、それにマッシュルームが入ります。	In go the tofu, peas, and mushrooms.
47	それを少々炒めます。	Fry it a bit.
48	それがすんだら、鍋にフタをします。	Once that's done we cover the pan.
49	火を弱めて中火にします。	Lower the heat to medium.
50	それを7分間煮込みます。	Let it simmer for seven minutes.

Day 6 チェックテスト

ふさわしい語句の意味を選ぼう。＜制限時間5分＞

1. be headed for：(A)〜に向かう　(B)〜を聞く　(C)〜が頭から離れない
2. grandmother：(A)女性の農夫　(B)祖母　(C)祖父
3. carry on：(A)〜に耐える　(B)〜を主張する　(C)〜を持ち込む
4. I'm afraid：(A)申し訳ありませんが　(B)その人の友人です
   (C)はっきり言いますが
5. all set：(A)すべて過ぎたこと　(B)全員着席　(C)準備ができて
6. aisle：(A)通路　(B)島　(C)座席
7. flight：(A)貨物　(B)飛行機の便　(C)飛行機
8. via：(A)ウイルス　(B)〜経由で　(C)〜へ向かって
9. leave：(A)出発する　(B)住む　(C)葉
10. boarding：(A)役員会　(B)搭乗　(C)離陸

11. crash：(A)溶ける　(B)プログラムが動かなくなる　(C)落下する
12. conflict：(A)融合　(B)コンクリート　(C)衝突
13. work：(A)作動する　(B)歩く　(C)遊ぶ
14. trouble：(A)旅行　(B)困難　(C)ドリブル
15. bet：(A)少し　(B)取るべき策　(C)コウモリ
16. reinstall：(A)〜を再インストールする　(B)嵐　(C)設置器具
17. disc：(A)危険　(B)ディスク　(C)輪
18. move：(A)映画　(B)携帯　(C)引っ越しする
19. anyway：(A)とにかく　(B)おそらく　(C)ひどく
20. extension：(A)内線　(B)外線　(C)携帯電話

21. Hi there.：(A)私です。　(B)そこです。　(C)こんにちは。
22. forget：(A)〜を手に入れる　(B)〜を渡す　(C)〜を忘れる
23. good：(A)効果的　(B)在庫切れ　(C)有効
24. expire：(A)期限が切れる　(B)体験する　(C)消火する

25. ring up：(A) 〜にリンクする　(B) 指輪をあげる
　　　　　　(C) 〜をレジに打つ
26. anyway：(A) 地下鉄　(B) ありえない　(C) とにかく
27. by the way：(A) 道に沿って　(B) ところで　(C) 途中で
28. add：(A) 広告　(B) 〜を加える　(C) 〜を除く
29. on special：(A) 取り立てて　(B) 特殊な　(C) 特別価格で
30. come to：(A)（金額が）〜になる　(B) 支払う　(C) 意味をなす

31. noise：(A) 鼻　(B) 物騒な　(C) 物音
32. probably：(A) あまり〜ない　(B) ことわざでは　(C) たぶん
33. believe：(A) 離れる　(B) 〜を信じる　(C) 葉をつける
34. Hold on：(A) 待て　(B)（電話を）切れ　(C) 手を上げろ
35. check out：(A) 〜を調べる　(B) 〜を比べる
　　　　　　 (C) 〜を取り上げる
36. cops：(A) 器　(B) 湯飲み　(C) 警察
37. burglar：(A) 強盗　(B) バーガー　(C) ブルガリア
38. careful：(A) 疑い深い　(B) 注意深い　(C) 元気な
39. cute：(A) かわいらしい　(B) やせ気味の　(C) 穏やかな
40. stray：(A) 野良犬　(B) 迷い猫　(C) ストロー

41. soy sauce：(A) 豆腐　(B) 醤油　(C) 味噌
42. mix：(A) 〜を混ぜ合わせる　(B) 最大限　(C) ジュース
43. wok：(A) 仕事　(B) 中華料理　(C) 中華鍋
44. minced：(A) みじん切りにした　(B) 地雷の　(C) 自分の
45. stir：(A) 階段を登る　(B) 〜を細切れにする　(C) 〜をかき混ぜる
46. bubble：(A) 石けんで洗う　(B) 凝固する　(C) 沸騰する
47. peas：(A) エンドウ豆　(B) ほうれん草　(C) にんじん
48. fry：(A) 飛ぶ　(B) 〜を炒める　(C) ハエ
49. pan：(A) 鍋　(B) フタ　(C) 釜
50. simmer：(A) 網焼きする　(B) ことこと煮える　(C) かき混ぜる

Week 1

チェックテスト解答

1. **(A)**	2. **(B)**	3. **(C)**	4. **(A)**	5. **(C)**
6. **(A)**	7. **(B)**	8. **(B)**	9. **(A)**	10. **(B)**
11. **(B)**	12. **(C)**	13. **(A)**	14. **(B)**	15. **(B)**
16. **(A)**	17. **(B)**	18. **(C)**	19. **(A)**	20. **(A)**
21. **(C)**	22. **(C)**	23. **(C)**	24. **(A)**	25. **(C)**
26. **(C)**	27. **(B)**	28. **(B)**	29. **(C)**	30. **(A)**
31. **(C)**	32. **(C)**	33. **(B)**	34. **(A)**	35. **(A)**
36. **(C)**	37. **(A)**	38. **(B)**	39. **(A)**	40. **(B)**
41. **(B)**	42. **(A)**	43. **(C)**	44. **(A)**	45. **(C)**
46. **(C)**	47. **(A)**	48. **(B)**	49. **(A)**	50. **(B)**

＜ワンポイント＞

　第1週のトレーニングはいかがでしたか？　やはり、Step 1「リスニング問題」がむずかしく感じられたでしょうか？　繰り返しになりますが、Part 3, 4の問題形式に慣れることが目的ですから、間違っても気にしないことです。

　問題形式に慣れるという点では、正答できたかどうかより、設問（Q1～Q6）を素早く理解できたことのほうが大事です。Part 3, 4, 7の設問は、合計108問。設問の意味がすぐにわからなければ、焦って間違うか（Part 3, 4）、解答時間が足りなくなります（Part 7）。

　ですから、Step 4「解答・解説チェック」の際は、設問の意味を正しく理解できていたかを確認することが大事です（選択肢は、正解の意味だけ確認すれば大丈夫です）。

　また、Step 5～6のトレーニングはいかがでしたか？　「トレーニング内容が少し物足りない」「もっとトレーニングしたい」と感じた方には、Week 2（50ページ）、Week 3（86ページ）、Week 4（122ページ）に応用トレーニングを紹介していますので、チャレンジしてみてください。

第 **3** 章

Week 2

Week 2
今週のトレーニング

Day 1〜 Day 5のトレーニング		
Step	内容	時間
1	リスニング問題（3問）	2分
2	リーディング問題（3問）	3分
3	文法・語彙問題（5問）	2分
4	解答・解説チェック	3分
5	直読直解トレーニング ① CD（英語）を聞いて、英文を目で追う。 ② CD（英語）を聞いて、日本語訳を目で追う。 ③ カンマ（,）、ピリオド（.）、スラッシュ（/）の単位で、英文の意味が理解できるか確認（理解できない部分は、日本語訳や語彙を参照）。	5〜15分
6	基本構文トレーニング ① 1文ずつCD（日本語・英語）を聞き、英語を数回音読。 ② 10文の英語を続けて音読（数回行なう）。 ③ テキストを縦に半分に折るなどして日本語訳を隠し、英語部分を見て意味がすぐにわかるか確認。 ④ 応用トレーニング「ルックアップ＆セイ」	5〜15分

＜ワンポイント＞

先週のトレーニングはいかがでしたか？ 少し物足りないと感じた方は、Step 6の④「応用トレーニング」として、以下を追加学習してください。テキストを見ないで基本構文を話す練習で、さらに学習効果が期待できます。

ルックアップ＆セイ	英文を音読したあと、顔を上げて（英文を見ずに）、英文を話す（小声か口パクでもOK）。言えなかった英文は何度か音読し、再チャレンジしてください。

Week 2

Day 1 会話文トレーニング

Step 1 リスニング問題
CDを聞いて、問題を解こう。＜制限時間2分＞

Q1. What is the man complaining about?
　　(A) His health
　　(B) His job
　　(C) His salary
　　(D) His wife

Q2. Who went to the chiropractor earlier?
　　(A) The man
　　(B) The woman
　　(C) The woman's friend
　　(D) The man's friend

Q3. Where is the chiropractor's office?
　　(A) Nearby
　　(B) In the next town
　　(C) In the same building
　　(D) Rather far from the speakers' office

Step 2　リーディング問題
英文を読んで、問題を解こう。＜制限時間3分＞

M:　My back is acting up again. I'd better go see a doctor.
W:　Grady, I know a good chiropractor. Maybe you should try him this time.

M:　The problem is, my insurance doesn't cover chiropractic services.
W:　He's not that expensive. He realigned my back, and I think it cost me only $100 for two sessions.
M:　A hundred bucks, eh. That's not too bad. I could afford that.

M:　So, where is his office located?
W:　It's actually just in the next block, in the Allen Building— seventh floor.

Q4.　What is the man's problem?
　　(A) His back hurts.
　　(B) His head hurts.
　　(C) He has no money.
　　(D) He has no insurance.

Q5.　What does the woman recommend?
　　(A) Going to a doctor
　　(B) Going to a chiropractor
　　(C) Getting better insurance
　　(D) Getting some medicine for pain

Q6.　What does the man say about insurance?
　　(A) It does not pay for a doctor.
　　(B) It does not pay for a chiropractor.
　　(C) It does not pay for some medicines.
　　(D) It does not pay the first $100 of a doctor's bill.

Step 3 文法・語彙問題

空欄にふさわしい語句を選ぼう。＜制限時間2分＞

Q7. My back is acting ----- again, and I'm going to see a doctor.
  (A) up
  (B) out
  (C) down
  (D) on

Q8. ----- better go see a doctor before my back gets worse.
  (A) I'll
  (B) I've
  (C) I'd
  (D) I'm

Q9. The chiropractor is good, so maybe you ----- try him this time.
  (A) do
  (B) shall
  (C) ought
  (D) should

Q10. I'm afraid my insurance doesn't ----- chiropractic services.
  (A) apply
  (B) make
  (C) cover
  (D) work

Q11. It cost me only $100 ----- two sessions, and I felt a lot better.
  (A) of
  (B) for
  (C) with
  (D) from

Step 4　解答・解説チェック

現時点での理解度を確認しよう。

問題文は、腰痛に悩む男性とカイロプラクターを推薦する女性の会話です。

1. 正解 **(A)**。質問：「男性は、何について不満を言っていますか？」。答え：「健康」。ヒント：My back is acting up again.
2. 正解 **(B)**。質問：「以前にカイロプラクターに行ったのは、誰ですか？」。答え：「女性」。ヒント：I know a good chiropractor., He realigned my back など。
3. 正解 **(A)**。質問：「カイロプラクターの診療所は、どこにありますか？」。答え：「近所」。ヒント：It's actually just in the next block
4. 正解 **(A)**。質問：「男性の問題は、何ですか？」。答え：「腰が痛む」。ヒント：My back is acting up again.
5. 正解 **(B)**。質問：「女性は、何を推薦していますか？」。答え：「カイロプラクターの所に行くこと」。ヒント：I know a good chiropractor. Maybe you should try him this time.
6. 正解 **(B)**。質問：「男性は、保険について何と言っていますか？」。答え：「それは、カイロプラクターへの支払いをしない」。ヒント：my insurance doesn't cover chiropractic services.
7. 正解 **(A)**。act up「(病気などが) 悪化する」の現在進行形を完成させる。
8. 正解 **(C)**。I'd better + 動詞「～したほうがよさそうだ」を完成させる。
9. 正解 **(D)**。「～してみたら」という提案の文意にするために、should を選ぶ。
10. 正解 **(C)**。文意から、cover「(保険などが) ～に適用される」を選ぶ。
11. 正解 **(B)**。「2回の診療で」という文意から、対象を表わす前置詞 for を選ぶ。

Step 5　直読直解トレーニング

速読速聴力を高めよう。

(※日本語訳は、英語の原文の順序どおりに記してあります。)

M:　My back is acting up again. I'd better go see a doctor.
　　また腰の調子が悪くなってきました。医者に行ったほうがいいようです。

W:　Grady, I know a good chiropractor.
　　グレイディ、いいカイロプラクターを知っています。
　　Maybe you should try him / this time.
　　彼を試してみたらいいでしょう、今回は。

M:　The problem is, my insurance doesn't cover / chiropractic services.
　　問題は、私の保険が適用されないのです、カイロプラクティックには。

W:　He's not that expensive. He realigned my back,
　　彼は、それほど高くありません。彼は、私の腰を整体してくれました、
　　and I think / it cost me only $100 / for two sessions.
　　そして思います、かかったのはたったの100ドルだ、2回の診療で。

M:　A hundred bucks, eh. That's not too bad. I could afford that.
　　えっ、100ドルですって。それなら、悪くないです。それなら、払えます。

M:　So, where is his office located?
　　それで、彼の治療所はどこにありますか？

W:　It's actually just in the next block,
　　ほら、すぐ隣のブロックの、
　　in the Allen Building — seventh floor.
　　アレンビルの―7階です。

語句

back：腰、背中	**act up**：悪化する
chiropractor：脊椎指圧師	**insurance**：保険
chiropractic：脊椎指圧療法	**expensive**：高額な
realign：～を再調整する	**session**：治療などの1回
buck：[口語] ドル	**afford**：経済的余裕がある

Step 6　基本構文トレーニング
文法・語彙力を高めよう。

51	また腰の調子が悪くなってきました。	My back is acting up again.
52	医者に行ったほうがいいようです。	I'd better go see a doctor.
53	今回は彼を試してみたらいいでしょう。	Maybe you should try him this time.
54	私の保険は、カイロプラクティックには適用されません。	My insurance doesn't cover chiropractic services.
55	彼は、それほど高くありません。	He's not that expensive.
56	私の腰を整体してくれました。	He realigned my back.
57	2回の診療でたったの100ドルしかかかりませんでした。	It cost me only $100 for two sessions.
58	それなら、悪くはありません。	That's not too bad.
59	それなら、払えます。	I could afford that.
60	彼の治療所はどこにありますか？	Where is his office located?

Week 2

Day 2 会話文トレーニング

Step 1 リスニング問題

CDを聞いて、問題を解こう。＜制限時間2分＞

Q1. Where are the speakers?
   (A) In a bank
   (B) In an office
   (C) In a store
   (D) In an elevator

Q2. Who is the man?
   (A) A customer
   (B) A baker
   (C) A cheese maker
   (D) A banker

Q3. What did the man give the woman?
   (A) Cinnamon rolls
   (B) Bread
   (C) Advice
   (D) Money

Step 2　リーディング問題
英文を読んで、問題を解こう。＜制限時間3分＞

W: Hello, sir. What can I get for you this morning?
M: I'd like a half loaf of the whole wheat, please. I want the one with sesame seeds on it. Give me a cinnamon roll, too, please.

W: And how would you like your bread sliced?
M: Make it those thick toast slices. Oh, and could I also get a cheese scone?
W: We have two kinds—cheese and chives, and cheese and onion.

W: That's $6.75. Out of $10, here's your change, sir.
M: Thanks very much. Take it easy.

Q4. How many items does the man buy?
　　(A) One
　　(B) Two
　　(C) Three
　　(D) Four

Q5. What does the woman ask the man about the bread?
　　(A) What kind he wants to buy
　　(B) How he wants to have it sliced
　　(C) How much he wants to buy
　　(D) Whether he wants to have it sliced

Q6. When does this conversation take place?
　　(A) After noon
　　(B) Before noon
　　(C) In the evening
　　(D) At night

Step 3　文法・語彙問題
空欄にふさわしい語句を選ぼう。＜制限時間2分＞

Q7. I want the one ------- sesame seeds on it, because it's so delicious.
(A) which
(B) with
(C) has
(D) of

Q8. ------- $10, here's your change: $3.25.
(A) Take out
(B) Spent
(C) Cost
(D) Out of

Q9. Take ------- easy and come back to see us.
(A) yourself
(B) it
(C) us
(D) the

Q10. I'd like a half ------- of the whole wheat bread this morning.
(A) loaf
(B) loft
(C) leaf
(D) load

Q11. How would you like your bread -------, thick or thin?
(A) to slice
(B) slicing
(C) sliced
(D) slice

Step 4　解答・解説チェック

現時点での理解度を確認しよう。

問題文は、パン屋での店員と客の会話です。

1. 正解 **(C)**。質問:「話し手は、どこにいますか?」。答え:「店の中」。ヒント:I'd like a half loaf ..., And how would you like your bread sliced?
2. 正解 **(A)**。質問:「男性は、誰ですか?」。答え:「客」。Hello, sir. What can I get for you this morning?
3. 正解 **(D)**。質問:「男性は、女性に何を渡しましたか?」。答え:「お金」。ヒント:That's $6.75. Out of $10, here's your change, sir.
4. 正解 **(C)**。質問:「男性は、何品買い物をしましたか?」。答え:「3品」。ヒント:a half loaf of the whole wheat, a cinnamon roll, a cheese scone
5. 正解 **(B)**。質問:「女性は、パンに関して男性にどのようなことを尋ねていますか?」。答え:「どのようにスライスするか」。ヒント:how would you like your bread sliced?
6. 正解 **(B)**。質問:「この会話が行なわれたのはいつですか?」。答え:「昼前」。ヒント:What can I get for you this morning?
7. 正解 **(B)**。文意から、「~付き」を表わす前置詞 with を選ぶ。(A)(C) は、which [that] has の形になる。
8. 正解 **(D)**。文意から、「~から」という意味で from とほぼ同義の Out of を選ぶ。
9. 正解 **(B)**。文意から、Take it easy.(ここでは、「それでは」という程度の別れ際のあいさつ)を完成させる。
10. 正解 **(A)**。loaf を選び、a half loaf of「半斤の~」を完成させる。
11. 正解 **(C)**。過去分詞 sliced を選び、like +(物)+ 形容詞・過去分詞「(物)が~(の状態)であることを好む」を完成させる。

Step 5　直読直解トレーニング

速読速聴力を高めよう。

(※日本語訳は、英語の原文の順序どおりに記してあります。)

W: Hello, sir. What can I get for you / this morning?
　　こんにちは、お客様。何を差し上げましょうか、今朝は？

M: I'd like a half loaf / of the whole wheat, please. I want /
　　半斤いただきます、ホールウィートを。欲しいです
　　the one with sesame seeds on it. Give me a cinnamon roll, too, please.
　　セサミシードのついたものが。シナモンロールも、お願いします。

W: And how would you like / your bread sliced?
　　それで、どういたしますか、パンの切り方は？

M: Make it those thick toast slices.
　　トースト用の厚切りに。
　　Oh, and could I also get a cheese scone?
　　あっ、チーズ・スコーンもいただけますか？

W: We have two kinds —cheese and chives, and cheese and onion.
　　2種類あります、チーズとチャイブ、それとチーズとオニオンです。

W: That's $6.75.
　　6ドル75セントになります。
　　Out of $10, here's your change, sir.
　　10ドルからで、こちらがおつりです、お客様。

M: Thanks very much. Take it easy.
　　どうもありがとう。それでは。

語句

- **loaf**：パン1斤
- **sesame**：ゴマ
- **cinnamon**：シナモン
- **cheese**：チーズ
- **chive**：チャイブ [ネギの一種]
- **whole wheat**：全粒小麦
- **seed**：種
- **thick**：厚い
- **scone**：スコーン [ビスケットのようなパン]
- **change**：おつり

Step 6　基本構文トレーニング

文法・語彙力を高めよう。

61	何を差し上げましょうか？	What can I get for you?
62	ホールウィートを半斤いただきます。	I'd like a half loaf of the whole wheat.
63	セサミシードのついたものがいいです。	I want the one with sesame seeds on it.
64	シナモンロールもお願いします。	Give me a cinnamon roll, too, please.
65	パンの切り方は、どういたしますか？	How would you like your bread sliced?
66	トースト用の厚切りにしてください。	Make it those thick toast slices.
67	チーズ・スコーンもいただけますか？	Could I also get a cheese scone?
68	6ドル75セントになります。	That's $6.75.
69	10ドルからですので、こちらがおつりです。	Out of $10, here's your change.
70	それでは。	Take it easy.

Day 3　会話文トレーニング

Step 1　リスニング問題
CDを聞いて、問題を解こう。＜制限時間2分＞

Q1. What are the people looking at?
(A) A handwritten letter
(B) A computer
(C) A map
(D) A newspaper

Q2. What does the woman think about spammers?
(A) They are easy to catch.
(B) They are becoming more stupid.
(C) They are getting smarter.
(D) They are easy to find.

Q3. Why do the people think the message is strange?
(A) It is filled with misspelled words.
(B) It looks very old-fashioned.
(C) It is written in a foreign language.
(D) It looks real.

Step 2　リーディング問題
英文を読んで、問題を解こう。＜制限時間3分＞

M: Have a look at this. What is all this? It looks like some sort of chain letter.
W: Who is this from? Have you read any of it? This is just bizarre.

M: My guess is it has to be some sort of spam, but it looks legitimate.
W: I wouldn't click on that link, though. You just never know.
M: So I should just delete it?

M: What's strange is it had the exact same format as the usual e-mail I get from Carson Graham Industries.
W: E-mail spammers are getting cleverer, I guess.

Q4. What does the woman think of the e-mail?
　　(A) It is humorous.
　　(B) It is rude.
　　(C) It is odd.
　　(D) It is not dangerous.

Q5. What does the e-mail contain?
　　(A) A link
　　(B) An attachment
　　(C) A photograph
　　(D) A telephone number

Q6. Why are Carson Graham Industries mentioned?
　　(A) They sometimes send spam.
　　(B) They sent the e-mail to the man.
　　(C) A spammer works for them.
　　(D) A spammer imitated their e-mail format.

Step 3　文法・語彙問題

空欄にふさわしい語句を選ぼう。＜制限時間2分＞

Q7. I'm not sure, but it looks like some ----- chain letter.
　　(A) sort
　　(B) sorts
　　(C) sort of
　　(D) sorts of

Q8. It looks -----, but I'll bet it's not.
　　(A) rightly
　　(B) legitimate
　　(C) typically
　　(D) spammer

Q9. I ----- click on that link if I were you.
　　(A) won't
　　(B) didn't
　　(C) mustn't
　　(D) wouldn't

Q10. What's strange is it had the ----- same format as the usual e-mail.
　　(A) just
　　(B) exactly
　　(C) exact
　　(D) justly

Q11. E-mail spammers are ----- cleverer, I guess.
　　(A) going
　　(B) putting
　　(C) doing
　　(D) getting

Step 4　解答・解説チェック

現時点での理解度を確認しよう。

問題文は、怪しい E メールを受け取って、思案する男女の会話です。

1. 正解 **(B)**。質問:「話し手たちは、何を見ていますか？」。答え:「コンピュータ」。ヒント : I wouldn't click on that link, though., So I should just delete it? など。
2. 正解 **(C)**。質問:「女性は、スパマーについてどう思っていますか？」。答え :「彼らは賢くなっている」。ヒント : E-mail spammers are getting cleverer, I guess.
3. 正解 **(D)**。質問:「話し手たちは、なぜメッセージが変だと思っていますか？」。答え:「実際のものと似ているから」。ヒント : What's strange is it had the exact same format as the usual e-mail
4. 正解 **(C)**。質問:「女性は E メールについて、どう思っていますか？」。答え:「奇妙」。ヒント : This is just bizarre.
5. 正解 **(A)**。質問:「E メールには、何が含まれていますか？」。答え :「リンク」。ヒント : I wouldn't click on that link
6. 正解 **(D)**。質問:「カーソン・グラハム工業が述べられているのは、なぜですか？」。答え:「スパマーが、そこの E メールの書式を真似ていた」。ヒント : it had the exact same format as the usual e-mail I get from Carson Graham Industries.
7. 正解 **(C)**。some sort of「〜の一種」を完成させる。
8. 正解 **(B)**。文意から、legitimate「適法の」を選ぶ。(A)「正しく」。(C)「典型的に」(副詞)。
9. 正解 **(D)**。if I were you「私があなた（の立場）だったら」なので、won't (will not) の仮定法 wouldn't を選ぶ。
10. 正解 **(C)**。文意から、same とともに、名詞 format を修飾する形容詞 exact を選ぶ。(B) は、exactly the same なら可。
11. 正解 **(D)**。get + 形容詞の比較級「ますます〜になる」の進行形を完成させる。

Step 5　直読直解トレーニング
速読速聴力を高めよう。
（※日本語訳は、英語の原文の順序どおりに記してあります。）

M: Have a look at this. What is all this?
　　これを見てください。これは、一体何でしょう？
　　It looks like / some sort of chain letter.
　　～のようです、チェーンレターの一種。
W: Who is this from? Have you read any of it?
　　これは、誰からですか？　それを読みましたか？
　　This is just bizarre.
　　これはなんとも奇妙です。

M: My guess is / it has to be some sort of spam,
　　私の想像では、スパムメールの類に違いありません、
　　but it looks legitimate.
　　しかし合法なようです。
W: I wouldn't click on that link, though. You just never know.
　　でも、私だったらそのリンクはクリックしません。わかりません。
M: So / I should just delete it?
　　では、それを削除してしまいましょうか？

M: What's strange is / it had the exact same format /
　　不思議なのは、それはまったく同じ形式だったことです、
　　as the usual e-mail / I get from Carson Graham Industries.
　　いつものEメールと、私がカーソン・グラハム工業から受け取る。
W: E-mail spammers are / getting cleverer, I guess.
　　スパムメール発信者は、ますます賢くなっている、と思います。

語句
have a look：見る　look like：～のようだ　sort of：一種の
chain letter：チェーンレター　bizarre：奇怪な　guess：想像
spam：広告メール　legitimate：適法の　delete：～を削除する　format：形式

Step 6　基本構文トレーニング
文法・語彙力を高めよう。

71	これを見てください。	Have a look at this.
72	これは、一体何でしょう？	What is all this?
73	チェーンレターの一種のようです。	It looks like some sort of chain letter.
74	これは、誰から来ましたか？	Who is this from?
75	私の想像では、それはスパムメールの類に違いありません。	My guess is it has to be some sort of spam.
76	それは、合法なようです。	It looks legitimate.
77	私だったら、そのリンクはクリックしません。	I wouldn't click on that link.
78	では、それを削除してしまいましょうか？	So I should just delete it?
79	不思議なのは、それがまったく同じ形式だったことです。	What's strange is it had the exact same format.
80	スパムメール発信者は、ますます賢くなっているのだと思います。	E-mail spammers are getting cleverer, I guess.

Day 4 会話文トレーニング

Step 1　リスニング問題

CD を聞いて、問題を解こう。＜制限時間2分＞

Q1. What are the people doing?
　　(A) Shopping
　　(B) Eating
　　(C) Working
　　(D) Fishing

Q2. What does the man like best?
　　(A) The potatoes
　　(B) The chicken
　　(C) The seafood
　　(D) The coconut sauce

Q3. What does the woman think of the prawns?
　　(A) She hates them.
　　(B) She loves them.
　　(C) She would never eat one.
　　(D) She thinks they have no taste.

Step 2　リーディング問題
英文を読んで、問題を解こう。＜制限時間3分＞

W: You must try the prawns here. They are fantastic.
M: You know, I'm not big on seafood. I think I'll stick with the chicken.

W: So how's your chicken then?
M: Not bad. The thing I love are these mashed potatoes. They're so light and fluffy.
W: Here, try just one prawn. I'm telling you these taste great.

W: I told you, didn't I? It's the coconut sauce that makes all the difference.
M: They are pretty delicious. I wish all seafood tasted this good. I'd eat it every day.

Q4. What does the woman recommend to the man?
   (A) Soup
   (B) Beef
   (C) Salad
   (D) Prawns

Q5. What does the man not like very much?
   (A) Seafood
   (B) Chicken
   (C) Coconut sauce
   (D) Mashed potatoes

Q6. What does the man finally agree to do?
   (A) To taste a prawn
   (B) To order the prawns
   (C) To taste the potatoes
   (D) To eat seafood every day

Step 3　文法・語彙問題
空欄にふさわしい語句を選ぼう。＜制限時間2分＞

Q7. You ----- try the prawns here, because they're delicious.
　　(A) need
　　(B) ought
　　(C) must
　　(D) have

Q8. You know, I'm not ----- on seafood.
　　(A) large
　　(B) big
　　(C) little
　　(D) good

Q9. Thanks, but I think I'll stick ----- the chicken.
　　(A) with
　　(B) up
　　(C) on
　　(D) at

Q10. It's the coconut sauce ----- makes all the difference.
　　(A) what
　　(B) it
　　(C) that
　　(D) so

Q11. I ----- all seafood tasted this good.
　　(A) wish
　　(B) want
　　(C) like
　　(D) hope

Step 4　解答・解説チェック

現時点での理解度を確認しよう。

問題文は、レストランで食事をしている男女の会話です。

1. 正解 **(B)**。質問：「話し手たちは、何をしていますか？」。答え：「食事」。ヒント：You must try the prawns here., I think I'll stick with the chicken. など。
2. 正解 **(A)**。質問：「男性がいちばん好きなのは、何ですか？」。答え：「ジャガイモ」。ヒント：The thing I love are these mashed potatoes.
3. 正解 **(B)**。質問：「女性は、エビをどう思っていますか？」。答え：「大好き」。ヒント：They are fantastic.
4. 正解 **(D)**。質問：「女性は、男性に何を勧めますか？」。答え：「エビ」。ヒント：You must try the prawns here.
5. 正解 **(A)**。質問：「男性があまり好まないものは、何ですか？」。答え：「シーフード」。ヒント：I'm not big on seafood.
6. 正解 **(A)**。質問：「男性は、最後に何をすることに同意しましたか？」。答え：「エビを味見すること」。ヒント：They are pretty delicious.
7. 正解 **(C)**。文意から、must + 動詞「ぜひ〜するように」を完成させる。(B) ought to、(D) have to なら可。
8. 正解 **(B)**。big on「〜が大好き」の否定形を完成させる。
9. 正解 **(A)**。stick with「〜のままでいる」を完成させる。
10. 正解 **(C)**。it's 〜 that 節「(節) なのは〜だ」の構文を完成させる。
11. 正解 **(A)**。all 以下の節の動詞が tasted（過去形）なので、現在の事実と異なる願望を表わす wish「〜だったらよかったのに」を選ぶ。

Step 5　直読直解トレーニング

速読速聴力を高めよう。

(※日本語訳は、英語の原文の順序どおりに記してあります。)

W: You must try the prawns here. They are fantastic.
　　ここのエビをぜひ食べてみてください。それらは、とってもおいしいです。

M: You know, I'm not big on seafood. I think / I'll stick with the chicken.
　　あの、シーフードは好きではありません。思います、チキンにしようと。

W: So / how's your chicken then?
　　それで、あなたのチキンはどうですか？

M: Not bad. The thing I love are / these mashed potatoes.
　　悪くありません。私が好きなのは、これらのマッシュポテトです。
　　They're so light and fluffy.
　　それらは、とてもあっさりして、ふかふかしています。

W: Here, try just one prawn. I'm telling you / these taste great.
　　はい、1つでいいからエビを食べて。本当に、すごくおいしいです。

W: I told you, didn't I? It's the coconut sauce /
　　言ったとおりでしょう？　ココナッツソースです、
　　that makes all the difference.
　　ひと味違うのは。

M: They are pretty delicious. I wish / all seafood tasted this good.
　　おいしいです。願います、シーフードがどれも、こんなにおいしいことを。
　　I'd eat it every day.
　　それを毎日食べるでしょう。

語句

try：〜を試す	**prawn**：エビ
big on：〜が大好き	**stick with**：〜に固執する
Not bad：悪くない	**mashed**：すりつぶした
light：あっさりした	**fluffy**：ふわふわした
taste great：おいしい	**difference**：違い

Step 6　基本構文トレーニング
文法・語彙力を高めよう。

81	ここのエビをぜひ食べてみてください。	You must try the prawns here.
82	それらは、とてもおいしいです。	They are fantastic.
83	あのね、私はシーフードはあまり好きではありません。	You know, I'm not big on seafood.
84	チキンにしておこうと思います。	I think I'll stick with the chicken.
85	私が好きなのは、これらのマッシュポテトです。	The thing I love are these mashed potatoes.
86	それらは、とてもあっさりして、ふかふかしています。	They're so light and fluffy.
87	本当に、それらはすごくおいしいです。	I'm telling you these taste great.
88	言ったとおりでしょう？	I told you, didn't I?
89	ひと味違うものにしているのは、ココナッツソースです。	It's the coconut sauce that makes all the difference.
90	シーフードがどれも、こんなにおいしかったらいいのに。	I wish all seafood tasted this good.

Day 5　説明文トレーニング

Step 1　リスニング問題
CDを聞いて、問題を解こう。＜制限時間2分＞

Q1. What is causing a problem?
　　(A) High temperatures
　　(B) High pollen levels
　　(C) Low pollen levels
　　(D) Low temperatures

Q2. Who will find the speech most useful?
　　(A) People taking care of babies
　　(B) People with broken bones
　　(C) People with allergies
　　(D) People taking care of older relatives

Q3. When does the speaker recommend taking a shower?
　　(A) Early in the morning
　　(B) Before you leave the house
　　(C) When you arrive home
　　(D) Late at night

Step 2　リーディング問題

英文を読んで、問題を解こう。＜制限時間3分＞

Pollen levels are now at their highest, and those who suffer from hay fever and other allergies caused by airborne allergens need relief. Besides the usual medicine, here are some tips to help you out:

-When arriving home, remove your shoes and clothes as soon as possible and change into fresh clothes. This helps reduce the time the pollen is attached to clothing and is in touch with your skin.

-Also, it's a good idea to take a shower the minute you come home, as pollen thrives in dry conditions. In other words, you can literally wash the pollen away with soap and water.

Q4.　How many allergies are named?
　　(A) One
　　(B) Two
　　(C) Three
　　(D) Four

Q5.　How is pollen referred to?
　　(A) As an allergy
　　(B) As an allergen
　　(C) As an irritation
　　(D) As an inconvenience

Q6.　What do both tips recommend?
　　(A) Taking medicine
　　(B) Washing with a special kind of soap
　　(C) Removing what causes the allergy
　　(D) Using air freshener during pollen season

Step 3　文法・語彙問題
空欄にふさわしい語句を選ぼう。＜制限時間2分＞

Q7. Here are some ----- to help you out when you don't feel well.
　　(A) chips
　　(B) advice
　　(C) tips
　　(D) suggestion

Q8. Remove your shoes and ----- as soon as possible.
　　(A) cloth
　　(B) close
　　(C) cloths
　　(D) clothes

Q9. When you come inside, immediately change ----- fresh clothes.
　　(A) over
　　(B) out
　　(C) into
　　(D) for

Q10. It is recommended that you take a shower ----- you come home.
　　(A) a minute
　　(B) an hour
　　(C) the minute
　　(D) the hour

Q11. It's ----- idea to take a shower as soon as you can.
　　(A) good
　　(B) a good
　　(C) the good
　　(D) to be good

Step 4　解答・解説チェック

現時点での理解度を確認しよう。

問題文は、花粉症に苦しむ人びとへのアドバイスです。

1. 正解 **(B)**。質問：「問題の原因になっていることは、何ですか？」。答え：「大量の花粉」。ヒント：Pollen levels are now at their highest
2. 正解 **(C)**。質問：「このスピーチが、もっとも役に立つのは誰ですか？」。答え：「アレルギーのある人」。ヒント：and those who suffer from hay fever and other allergies caused by airborne allergens need relief.
3. 正解 **(C)**。質問：「話し手は、いつシャワーを浴びることを勧めていますか？」。答え：「帰宅時」。ヒント：it's a good idea to take a shower the minute you come home
4. 正解 **(A)**。質問：「何種類のアレルギーが、記述されていますか？」。答え：「1種類」。ヒント：hay fever
5. 正解 **(B)**。質問：「花粉は、何と見なされていますか？」。答え：「アレルギー誘発物質」。ヒント：2つの助言で、pollen を排除することが述べられている。
6. 正解 **(C)**。質問：「両方の助言で勧めていることは、何ですか？」。答え：「アレルギーの原因となるものを排除する」。ヒント：remove your shoes and clothes, it's a good idea to take a shower the minute you come home
7. 正解 **(C)**。Here are some のあとなので、複数形の名詞がくる。文意から、tips「ヒント」を選ぶ。(B)「アドバイス」(不可算名詞) は、Here is some advice. なら可。(D)「提案」(名詞・単数形) は、suggestions about helping なら可。
8. 正解 **(D)**。文意から、clothes「衣服」(複数形) を選ぶ。
9. 正解 **(C)**。change into「~に着替える」を完成させる。
10. 正解 **(C)**。文意から、the minute「~するやいなや」を選ぶ。
11. 正解 **(B)**。It's a good idea to + 動詞「~するのはいい考えだ」を完成させる。

Step 5　直読直解トレーニング

速読速聴力を高めよう。
（※日本語訳は、英語の原文の順序どおりに記してあります。）

Pollen levels are / now at their highest, and those who suffer /
花粉量は、今が最高潮で、悩まされている人は、
from hay fever and other allergies / caused by airborne allergens /
花粉症やその他のアレルギーに、空中に浮遊するアレルギー源が原因の、
need relief. Besides the usual medicine, here are some tips to help you out:
対策が必要です。通常の薬品に加えて、あなたに役立つヒントがあります。

-When arriving home, remove your shoes and clothes / as soon as possible /
　家に着いたら、靴や服を脱いでください、できるだけ速やかに、
　and change into fresh clothes. This helps / reduce the time /
　そして新しい服に着替えてください。これが役立ちます、時間を減らすのに、
　the pollen is attached to clothing / and is in touch with your skin.
　花粉が服に付着して、そして肌に触れている。

-Also, it's a good idea / to take a shower / the minute you come home,
　また、いい考えです、シャワーを浴びるのは、帰宅直後に、
　as pollen thrives / in dry conditions. In other words,
　花粉は活発になるので、乾燥した状態で。つまり、
　you can literally wash the pollen away / with soap and water.
　文字どおり花粉を洗い流せるのです、石けんと水で。

語句			
pollen：花粉		**suffer**：苦しむ	
hay fever：花粉症		**allergy**：アレルギー	
caused by：〜が原因の		**airborne**：空気で運ばれる	
relief：救済		**besides**：〜のほかに	
thrive：活発になる		**literally**：文字どおりに	

Step 6　基本構文トレーニング

文法・語彙力を高めよう。

91	花粉量は、今が最高潮です。	Pollen levels are now at their highest.
92	花粉症に悩まされている人は、対策が必要です。	Those who suffer from hay fever need relief.
93	あなたに役立ついくつかのヒントがあります。	Here are some tips to help you out.
94	できるだけ速やかに、靴や服を脱いでください。	Remove your shoes and clothes as soon as possible.
95	新しい服に着替えてください。	Change into fresh clothes.
96	これは、花粉が服に付着している時間を減らすのに役立ちます。	This helps reduce the time the pollen is attached.
97	シャワーを浴びるのは、いい考えです。	It's a good idea to take a shower.
98	帰宅直後にシャワーを浴びてください。	Take a shower the minute you come home.
99	花粉は、乾燥した状態で活発に成長をします。	Pollen thrives in dry conditions.
100	花粉を石けんと水で洗い流してください。	Wash the pollen away with soap and water.

Day 6 チェックテスト

ふさわしい語句の意味を選ぼう。＜制限時間5分＞

1. back：(A) 腰　(B) 腹　(C) 足の裏
2. act up：(A) 演じきる　(B) 悪化する　(C) 持ち上げる
3. chiropractor：(A) 化学分析士　(B) 医療介護士　(C) 脊椎指圧師
4. insurance：(A) 投資　(B) 借金　(C) 保険
5. chiropractic：(A) 筋肉トレーニング　(B) 脊椎指圧療法　(C) 溶解性プラスチック
6. expensive：(A) 高額な　(B) 延長の　(C) 安価な
7. realign：(A) ～を購入する　(B) ～を再調整する　(C) ～を終了する
8. session：(A) 治療などの1回　(B) 治療などの手始め　(C) 治療などの遅れ
9. buck：(A) 通貨　(B) 紙幣　(C) ドル
10. afford：(A) 時間的余裕がある　(B) スペースの余裕がある　(C) 経済的余裕がある

11. loaf：(A) パン1斤　(B) 葉っぱ　(C) 屋根
12. whole wheat：(A) ライ麦　(B) 大麦　(C) 全粒小麦
13. sesame：(A) サラミ　(B) ゴマ　(C) 同一の
14. seed：(A) 種　(B) 追求する　(C) 皮
15. cinnamon：(A) シナモン　(B) 映画　(C) シナリオ
16. thick：(A) 芸　(B) 暗い　(C) 厚い
17. cheese：(A) チェス　(B) チーズ　(C) 小切手
18. scone：(A) スコーン　(B) コーン　(C) ～を叱る
19. chive：(A) 子供　(B) 泥棒　(C) チャイブ
20. change：(A) 為替　(B) 紙幣　(C) おつり

21. have a look：(A) 見る　(B) 幸運を得る　(C) 情報を漏らす
22. look like：(A) 好きそうだ　(B) 見えそうだ　(C) ～のようだ

23. sort of：(A) 上質の　(B) 一種の　(C) 変わった
24. chain letter：(A) 手紙を交換する　(B) 鎖文字　(C) チェーンレター
25. bizarre：(A) 正当な　(B) 奇怪な　(C) 素敵な
26. guess：(A) 予知　(B) 想像　(C) 警告
27. spam：(A) 回転　(B) 間隔　(C) 広告メール
28. legitimate：(A) 適法の　(B) 違法の　(C) 州法の
29. delete：(A) ～を削除する　(B) ～を推薦する　(C) ～を追加する
30. format：(A) プラットホーム　(B) 形式　(C) マットレス

31. try：(A) ～に逆らう　(B) ～を試す　(C) ～を料理する
32. prawn：(A) エビ　(B) 道化師　(C) タコ
33. big on：(A) ～をたくさん持っている　(B) ～に興味がある
　　　　　(C) ～が大好き
34. stick with：(A) ～が張り付く　(B) ～に固執する　(C) ～を所有する
35. Not bad：(A) 悪くない　(B) とても悪い　(C) ほめられない
36. mashed：(A) 山盛りにした　(B) すりつぶした　(C) 練りあげた
37. light：(A) 味が薄い　(B) 甘い　(C) あっさりした
38. fluffy：(A) 熱々の　(B) ふわふわした　(C) 湯気の出た
39. taste great：(A) おいしい　(B) たくさん食べる　(C) 趣味がいい
40. difference：(A) 困難　(B) 距離　(C) 違い

41. pollen：(A) 花粉　(B) 花弁　(C) 茎
42. suffer：(A) 驚く　(B) 苦しむ　(C) 安らぐ
43. hay fever：(A) 熱中　(B) 高熱　(C) 花粉症
44. allergy：(A) エネルギー　(B) アレルギー　(C) 警告
45. caused by：(A) ～だが　(B) ～が原因の　(C) ～から成る
46. airborne：(A) 空気で運ばれる　(B) 空気で膨らんだ　(C) 気球の
47. relief：(A) 彫刻　(B) 作風　(C) 救済
48. besides：(A) ～の他に　(B) ～の脇に　(C) ～のうしろに
49. thrive：(A) 盗む　(B) 停滞する　(C) 活発になる
50. literally：(A) 文学の　(B) リットル単位で　(C) 文字どおりに

チェックテスト解答

1. **(A)**	2. **(B)**	3. **(C)**	4. **(C)**	5. **(B)**
6. **(A)**	7. **(B)**	8. **(A)**	9. **(C)**	10. **(C)**
11. **(A)**	12. **(C)**	13. **(B)**	14. **(A)**	15. **(A)**
16. **(C)**	17. **(B)**	18. **(A)**	19. **(C)**	20 **(C)**
21. **(A)**	22. **(C)**	23. **(B)**	24. **(C)**	25. **(B)**
26. **(B)**	27. **(C)**	28. **(A)**	29. **(A)**	30. **(B)**
31. **(B)**	32. **(A)**	33. **(C)**	34. **(B)**	35. **(A)**
36. **(B)**	37. **(C)**	38. **(B)**	39. **(A)**	40. **(C)**
41. **(A)**	42. **(B)**	43. **(C)**	44. **(B)**	45. **(B)**
46. **(A)**	47. **(C)**	48. **(A)**	49. **(C)**	50. **(C)**

<ワンポイント>

　第2週のトレーニングはいかがでしたか？　設問（Q1〜Q6）を素早く理解できるようになってきましたか？　設問が素早く理解できるようになってきたら、問題形式に慣れてきたと考えていいと思います。

　しかし、問題形式には慣れてきたけれど、「英語がさっぱり聞き取れない」という方も多いはずです。リスニング上達のコツは、いきなり母国語のように100%聞き取れることを期待しないこと。70%聞き取れたら十分ぐらいの気持ちで「リラックスして聞く」ことです。

　わからないところがあっても、気にしない。わからないところに意識を向けるのではなく、わかったところから想像する。いい力の加減で聞きましょう。リスニング力は、想像力。会話やスピーチの場面（WhoとWhere）を想像しながら聞き、問題を解きながら、わからなかったところも想像してみましょう。

第 **4** 章

Week 3

Week 3
今週のトレーニング

Day 1〜 Day 5のトレーニング			
Step	内容		時間
1	リスニング問題（3問）		2分
2	リーディング問題（3問）		3分
3	文法・語彙問題（5問）		2分
4	解答・解説チェック		3分
5	直読直解トレーニング		5〜15分
	①	CD（英語）を聞いて、英文を目で追う。	
	②	CD（英語）を聞いて、日本語訳を目で追う。	
	③	カンマ（,）、ピリオド（.）、スラッシュ（/）の単位で、英文の意味が理解できるか確認（理解できない部分は、日本語訳や語彙を参照）。	
6	基本構文トレーニング		5〜15分
	①	1文ずつCD（日本語・英語）を聞き、英語を数回音読。	
	②	10文の英語を続けて音読（数回行なう）。	
	③	テキストを縦に半分に折るなどして日本語訳を隠し、英語部分を見て意味がすぐにわかるか確認。	
	④	応用トレーニング「ルックアップ＆セイ」「音読筆写」	

＜ワンポイント＞

　先週の応用トレーニング「ルックアップ＆セイ」（50ページ）を、試してみましたか？　どうしても顔を上げて言えない基本構文は、音読筆写をしてみると、しっかり覚えることができます。

音読筆写	英文を声に出しながら、スピードを上げて5回書き写します（字は乱れてOK）。終了したら、顔を上げ、英語を話します（言えなかったら、あと2回音読筆写）。

Week 3

Day 1 会話文トレーニング

Step 1 リスニング問題
CDを聞いて、問題を解こう。＜制限時間2分＞

Q1. What is the man most concerned about?
　　(A) The contract and the bonus
　　(B) His career
　　(C) His wife and son
　　(D) His aging parents

Q2. What does the woman want to do?
　　(A) Hire the man
　　(B) Give the man more money
　　(C) Say good-bye to the man
　　(D) Talk to the man's wife

Q3. What will the man and woman do sometime later?
　　(A) Work for the same company
　　(B) Talk again
　　(C) Sign a contract
　　(D) Meet the woman's boss

Step 2　リーディング問題
英文を読んで、問題を解こう。＜制限時間3分＞

W: It looks like we disagree only on the length of the contract and the bonus clauses.
M: Even so, I really must insist on at least a three-year deal. After all, I'd be uprooting my family. With my son entering high school, I want to know for sure where I'll be the next three years.

W: Two years is the best I can do.
M: Then that may be a deal breaker. My family comes first.
W: I sympathize with you, but my hands are tied.

W: I'll talk to my supervisors and see if they will budge on this.
M: I'd appreciate that.

Q4. How many points have the speakers not agreed on?
　(A) One　　　　　　　　　(B) Two
　(C) Three　　　　　　　　(D) Four

Q5. What does the man say about the contract that is offered to him?
　(A) It is too short.
　(B) It is too long.
　(C) It does not include family benefits.
　(D) It does not provide enough salary.

Q6. How does the woman end the conversation?
　(A) She will see if the contract can be changed.
　(B) She will change the contract.
　(C) She is sorry that she cannot hire the man.
　(D) She will introduce the man to her supervisors.

Step 3　文法・語彙問題

空欄にふさわしい語句を選ぼう。＜制限時間2分＞

Q7. I must insist ----- a three-year deal before I can accept your offer.
　　(A) to
　　(B) in
　　(C) on
　　(D) of

Q8. If I took this job in Hong Kong, I'd be ----- my family.
　　(A) overturning
　　(B) uprooting
　　(C) overthrowing
　　(D) upbringing

Q9. ----- that may be a deal breaker if we can't agree on the bonus.
　　(A) Then
　　(B) When
　　(C) Unless
　　(D) Since

Q10. I understand completely, and I ----- with you.
　　(A) sympathy
　　(B) sympathetic
　　(C) sympathize
　　(D) sympathetically

Q11. My ----- are tied, so there is nothing I can do about it.
　　(A) feet
　　(B) hands
　　(C) legs
　　(D) fingers

Step 4　解答・解説チェック

現時点での理解度を確認しよう。

問題文は、雇用契約の内容に関して交渉する男女の会話です。

1. 正解 **(C)**。質問:「男性がもっとも懸念していることは、何ですか?」。答え:「彼の妻と息子」。ヒント:My family comes first.
2. 正解 **(A)**。質問:「女性がしたいことは、何ですか?」。答え:「男性を採用する」。ヒント:I'll talk to my supervisors and see if they will budge on this.
3. 正解 **(B)**。質問:「男性と女性がのちほど行なうことは、何ですか?」。答え:「再び話す」。ヒント:I'll talk to my supervisors and see if they will budge on this., I'd appreciate that.
4. 正解 **(B)**。質問:「話し手が同意にいたっていないのは、何点ですか?」。答え:「2点」。ヒント:we disagree only on the length of the contract and the bonus clauses.
5. 正解 **(A)**。質問:「男性は、提示された契約について何と言っていますか?」。答え:「(契約期間が)短すぎる」。ヒント:must insist on at least a three-year deal.
6. 正解 **(A)**。質問:「女性は、どのように会話を締めくくっていますか?」。答え:「契約内容の変更が可能か調べてみる」。ヒント:and see if they will budge on this.
7. 正解 **(C)**。insist on「~を主張する」、「~は譲れない」を完成させる。
8. 正解 **(B)**。選択肢はすべて動詞の現在分詞。uprooting を選び、I'd be uprooting「私は、~を転居させる」を完成させる。
9. 正解 **(A)**。if + 条件節があるので、「そうなったら」を意味する副詞 Then を選ぶ。
10. 正解 **(C)**。sympathize with「~に同情する」を完成させる。
11. 正解 **(B)**。one's hands are tied「(制約を受けていて)どうすることもできない」を完成させる。

Step 5　直読直解トレーニング

速読速聴力を高めよう。
（※日本語訳は、英語の原文の順序どおりに記してあります。）

W: It looks like / we disagree / only on the length of the contract /
　　〜ようです、われわれは合意できない、契約期間だけが、
　　and the bonus clauses.
　　それとボーナス条項に。

M: Even so, I really must insist / on at least a three-year deal.
　　そうだとしても、どうしても譲れません、短くとも3年契約という点は。
　　After all, I'd be uprooting my family. With my son entering high school,
　　というのも、私は家族を転居させることになります。息子が高校入学で、
　　I want to know for sure / where I'll be / the next three years.
　　確実に知りたいのです、どこにいることになるかを、これからの3年間。

W: Two years is the best / I can do.
　　2年が精一杯です、私にできる。

M: Then / that may be a deal breaker. My family comes first.
　　では、それで交渉決裂かもしれません。私の家族が最優先です。

W: I sympathize with you, but my hands are tied.
　　あなたに同情します、でも私にはどうにもなりません。

W: I'll talk to my supervisors / and see if they will budge / on this.
　　上層部に相談します、そして彼らが譲歩するか確かめてみます、この点を。

M: I'd appreciate that.
　　感謝します。

語句		
disagree：意見が合わない		**length**：長さ
contract：契約		**clause**：条項
insist：要求する		**deal**：契約
uproot：〜を引っ越しさせる		**supervisor**：管理者
budge：意見を変える		**appreciate**：〜を感謝する

Step 6　基本構文トレーニング
文法・語彙力を高めよう。

101	3年契約は譲れません。	I must insist on a three-year deal.
102	私は家族を転居させることになります。	I'd be uprooting my family.
103	どこにいることになるか知りたいのです。	I want to know where I'll be.
104	2年が私にできる精一杯です。	Two years is the best I can do.
105	では、それで交渉決裂かもしれません。	Then that may be a deal breaker.
106	私の家族が最優先です。	My family comes first.
107	あなたに同情します。	I sympathize with you.
108	私には、どうすることもできません。	My hands are tied.
109	彼らがこの点を譲歩するか確かめてみます。	I'll see if they will budge on this.
110	それを感謝します。	I'd appreciate that.

Day 2 会話文トレーニング

Step 1 リスニング問題
CDを聞き、問題を解こう。＜制限時間2分＞

Q1. Where does the conversation take place?
　　(A) In an office
　　(B) In a store
　　(C) At the beach
　　(D) At a swimming pool

Q2. Who is the woman?
　　(A) A customer
　　(B) A pro surfer
　　(C) A salesperson
　　(D) A reporter

Q3. At the end, what does the woman tell the man?
　　(A) When to return to pick up his things
　　(B) Where to find what he wants
　　(C) How long it will take to get his order
　　(D) How much to pay

Step 2　リーディング問題
英文を読んで、問題を解こう。＜制限時間３分＞

W: Hi, there. Are you looking for something in particular?
M: Yes, I'm curious about your beach sandals. All of these are half-off, correct?

W: So that's everything for today, sir?
M: Yes and no. For today, yes. But I was wondering if you'll get more Kunda Beachwear.
W: That line has been discontinued. Sorry. I believe they were bought out by ProSurfer. I can give you the ProSurfer catalogue, though. There's an extra copy around here somewhere.

W: Your total comes to $54.97.
M: Oh, wait. I have a discount coupon that's still good.

Q4. Who is the woman's employer?
(A) A shop
(B) Kunda Beachwear
(C) ProSurfer
(D) A sandal maker

Q5. What is the man interested in?
(A) Kunda and ProSurfer products
(B) Sandals and Kunda Beachwear
(C) Beachwear catalogues
(D) Sandals only

Q6. According to the woman, what is NOT available?
(A) ProSurfer products　　(B) Beach sandals
(C) A discount　　(D) Kunda Beachwear

Step 3　文法・語彙問題
空欄にふさわしい語句を選ぼう。＜制限時間 2 分＞

Q7. Welcome! Are you looking for something ----- particular?
(A) for
(B) of
(C) in
(D) on

Q8. I'm ----- about your beach sandals there in the window.
(A) curious
(B) curiosity
(C) a curiosity
(D) the curious

Q9. I was wondering ----- you'll get more Kunda Beachwear.
(A) that
(B) if
(C) so
(D) until

Q10. That line has been -----, so we don't sell them now.
(A) stopped making
(B) gone out
(C) died
(D) discontinued

Q11. I have a ----- coupon that's still good, I think.
(A) discount
(B) cheap
(C) guarantee
(D) saving

Step 4　解答・解説チェック

現時点での理解度を確認しよう。

問題文は、買い物客と店員のやり取りです。

1. 正解 **(B)**。質問：「この会話は、どこで行なわれていますか？」。答え：「店の中」。ヒント：Hi, there. Are you looking for something in particular?
2. 正解 **(C)**。質問：「女性は、どんな人ですか？」。答え：「販売員」。ヒント：Q1 同様。
3. 正解 **(D)**。質問：「会話の最後で、女性は男性に何を伝えていますか？」。答え：「支払う金額」。ヒント：Your total comes to $54.97.
4. 正解 **(A)**。質問：「この女性は、どこに勤めていますか？」。答え：「お店」。ヒント：Q1 同様。
5. 正解 **(B)**。質問：「男性が関心があるのは、何ですか？」。答え：「サンダルとクンダのビーチウエア」。ヒント：I'm curious about your beach sandals., I was wondering if you'll get more Kunda Beachwear.
6. 正解 **(D)**。質問：「この女性によると、手に入らない物は何ですか？」。答え：「クンダのビーチウエア」。ヒント：That line has been discontinued.
7. 正解 **(C)**。something in particular「何か特定の物」を完成させる。
8. 正解 **(A)**。curious about「～が気になる」を完成させる。
9. 正解 **(B)**。I was wondering + if 節「～かな、と思っていました」という、間接的な問いかけの文を完成させる。
10. 正解 **(D)**。「生産中止になった」という文意から、discontinue「～を止める」の過去分詞 discontinued を選び、受動態を完成させる。
11. 正解 **(A)**。discount coupon「割引クーポン」を完成させる。

Step 5　直読直解トレーニング
速読速聴力を高めよう。
(※日本語訳は、英語の原文の順序どおりに記してあります。)

W:　Hi, there. Are you looking for / something in particular?
　　こんにちは。お探しですか、特に何か？
M:　Yes, I'm curious / about your beach sandals.
　　ええ、興味があります、こちらのビーチサンダルに。
　　All of these are half-off, correct?
　　それらは、すべて半額ですよね？

W:　So / that's everything for today, sir?
　　では、本日はそれだけでよろしいですか、お客様？
M:　Yes and no. For today, yes.
　　どちらとも言えません。今日のところは、そうです。
　　But I was wondering / if you'll get more Kunda Beachwear.
　　でも、〜かなと思って、クンダのビーチウエアはもっと入荷になる。
W:　That line has been discontinued. Sorry. I believe /
　　そのシリーズは、生産中止になりました。申し訳ありません。〜のはずです、
　　they were bought out / by ProSurfer. I can give you / the ProSurfer
　　彼らは買収された、プロサーファー社に。差し上げることはできます、
　　catalogue, though. There's an extra copy / around here somewhere.
　　プロサーファーのカタログを。予備のコピーがあります、どこかこの辺に。

W:　Your total / comes to $54.97.
　　合計で、54ドル97セントになります。
M:　Oh, wait. I have a discount coupon / that's still good.
　　ちょっと待って。割引クーポンがあります、まだ有効な。

語句

in particular：特に　　**curious about**：〜に興味がある　　**half-off**：半額の
wonder if：〜かなと思う　　**discontinue**：〜を中止する　　**buy out**：〜を買収する
extra：余分の　　**around here**：この辺　　**somewhere**：どこか　　**total**：合計

Step 6　基本構文トレーニング
文法・語彙力を高めよう。

111	特に何かお探しですか？	Are you looking for something in particular?
112	こちらのビーチサンダルに興味があります。	I'm curious about your beach sandals.
113	それらは、すべて半額ですよね？	All of these are half-off, correct?
114	本日は、それだけでよろしいですか？	That's everything for today?
115	クンダのビーチウエアは、もっと入荷になるのかと思って。	I was wondering if you'll get more Kunda Beachwear.
116	その商品の生産は中止になりました。	That line has been discontinued.
117	彼らは、プロサーファー社に買収されたと思います。	I believe they were bought out by ProSurfer.
118	プロサーファーのカタログを差し上げることはできますが。	I can give you the ProSurfer catalogue, though.
119	どこかこの辺に、予備のコピーがあります。	There's an extra copy around here somewhere.
120	まだ有効な割引クーポンがあります。	I have a discount coupon that's still good.

Week 3

Day 3 会話文トレーニング

Step 1 リスニング問題
CDを聞いて、問題を解こう。＜制限時間2分＞

Q1. Who are the people?
　　(A) A husband and wife
　　(B) A service rep and a customer
　　(C) A pilot and flight attendant
　　(D) A teacher and a student

Q2. Whom did the man call first?
　　(A) His wife
　　(B) His boss
　　(C) His son
　　(D) His friend

Q3. What did the woman ask the man for?
　　(A) His wallet
　　(B) His birth date
　　(C) Some numbers
　　(D) His wife's telephone number

Step 2　リーディング問題

英文を読んで、問題を解こう。＜制限時間３分＞

W: Beta Customer Service. Wanda speaking. How may I help you today?
M: Yes, I need to cancel all my credit cards. I lost my wallet.

W: OK, sir. Do you have those card numbers available?
M: Actually, I do. I called my wife this morning to get them from her.
W: That makes things much easier. Please go ahead with the first card you wish to cancel.

W: You're done. All your cards have been canceled. We'll flag any charges showing up from yesterday on. Your replacement cards will be sent out tomorrow to your home address.
M: Thank you very much. That's a great relief!

Q4. Why has the man called Beta Customer Service?
(A) He has lost his credit cards.
(B) He does not like their service.
(C) He wants to apply for a different credit card.
(D) He wants to find out his credit card numbers

Q5. From this conversation, what is known about the man?
(A) He has many credit card accounts.
(B) He has children.
(C) He is married.
(D) He works at home.

Q6. How does the man sound at the end of the conversation?
(A) Worried   (B) Grateful
(C) Unhappy   (D) Excited

Step 3　文法・語彙問題
空欄にふさわしい語句を選ぼう。＜制限時間2分＞

Q7. I need to cancel ----- my credit cards as soon as possible.
　　(A) all
　　(B) every one
　　(C) total
　　(D) each one

Q8. Please ----- ahead with the first card and I'll write down the number.
　　(A) do
　　(B) make
　　(C) say
　　(D) go

Q9. All your cards have been -----, so you don't have to worry.
　　(A) cancel
　　(B) canceling
　　(C) canceled
　　(D) cancellation

Q10. We'll flag ----- charges showing up from yesterday on.
　　(A) any
　　(B) another
　　(C) what
　　(D) at all

Q11. Your replacement cards will be sent ----- tomorrow.
　　(A) to
　　(B) out
　　(C) of
　　(D) with

Step 4　解答・解説チェック
現時点での理解度を確認しよう。

問題文は、財布をなくした男性が、クレジットカードを停止するための連絡をしている場面です。

1. 正解 **(B)**。質問：「話し手たちは、どんな人ですか？」。答え：「顧客サービス担当者と客」。ヒント：Beta Customer Service., Yes, I need to cancel all my credit cards.
2. 正解 **(A)**。質問：「男性は、最初に誰に電話をかけましたか？」。答え：「彼の妻」。ヒント：I called my wife
3. 正解 **(C)**。質問：「女性は、男性に何を尋ねましたか？」。答え：「ある数字」。ヒント：Do you have those card numbers available?
4. 正解 **(A)**。質問：「男性は、なぜベータ顧客サービスに電話をかけたのですか？」。答え：「クレジットカードを紛失した」。ヒント：I need to cancel all my credit cards. I lost my wallet.
5. 正解 **(C)**。質問：「会話から、男性についてどんなことがわかりますか？」。答え：「結婚している」。ヒント：I called my wife
6. 正解 **(B)**。質問：「会話の最後で、男性の口調はどうですか？」。答え：「感謝している」。ヒント：Thank you very much. That's a great relief!
7. 正解 **(A)**。文意から、all「すべての」を選ぶ。
8. 正解 **(D)**。go ahead with「～から始める」を完成させる。
9. 正解 **(C)**。カードは、「解約される」ものなので、canceled（過去分詞）を選び、受動態を完成させる。
10. 正解 **(A)**。文意から、any「どんな～」を選ぶ。
11. 正解 **(B)**。文意から、out を選び、send out「～を郵送する」の受動態を完成させる。

Step 5　直読直解トレーニング

速読速聴力を高めよう。

（※日本語訳は、英語の原文の順序どおりに記してあります。）

W: Beta Customer Service. Wanda speaking. How may I help you today?
ベータ顧客サービス。ワンダです。本日は、どのようなご用件でしょうか？

M: Yes, I need to cancel / all my credit cards.
はい、解約しなければなりません、私のすべてのクレジットカードを。
I lost my wallet.
財布をなくしました。

W: OK, sir. Do you have / those card numbers available?
承知しました、お客様。お持ちですか、それらのカード番号をお手元に？

M: Actually, I do. I called my wife this morning / to get them from her.
はい、あります。今朝、家内に電話して、彼女から教えてもらいました。

W: That makes / things much easier. Please go ahead / with the first card /
それなら、手続きはずっと簡単です。始めてください、1枚目のカードから
you wish to cancel.
解約を希望される。

W: You're done. All your cards have been canceled. We'll flag any charges /
終わりです。カードはすべて解約されました。すべての請求を凍結します、
showing up / from yesterday on. Your replacement cards /
発生した、昨日以降に。あなたの再発行カードは
will be sent out tomorrow / to your home address.
明日発送されます、ご自宅宛に。

M: Thank you very much. That's a great relief!
ありがとうございます。これでひと安心です！

語句
wallet：財布　**available**：利用できる　**actually**：実際に　**go ahead**：話を進める
flag：〜を合図で停止させる　**charge**：料金　**show up**：現われる
replacement card：再発行カード　**send out**：〜を郵送する　**great relief**：大きな安堵

Step 6　基本構文トレーニング

文法・語彙力を高めよう。

121	私のすべてのクレジットカードを解約しなければなりません。	I need to cancel all my credit cards.
122	財布をなくしました。	I lost my wallet.
123	それらのカード番号はお手元にありますか？	Do you have those card numbers available?
124	それなら、手続きはずっと簡単です。	That makes things much easier.
125	最初のカードから始めてください。	Please go ahead with the first card.
126	これで終わりです。	You're done.
127	あなたのカードはすべて解約されました。	All your cards have been canceled.
128	われわれは、昨日以降に発生した請求を、すべて凍結します。	We'll flag any charges showing up from yesterday on.
129	あなたの再発行カードは、明日発送されます。	Your replacement cards will be sent out tomorrow.
130	これでひと安心です！	That's a great relief!

Day 4 会話文トレーニング

Step 1　リスニング問題

CD を聞いて、問題を解こう。＜制限時間 2 分＞

Q1. Where did the conversation take place?
- (A) In Rachel's apartment
- (B) In a television studio
- (C) In a newspaper office
- (D) In a movie theater

Q2. Why does the woman want to see the man again?
- (A) He is her boss.
- (B) He is her fiancé.
- (C) He is a good guest.
- (D) He is a well-known politician.

Q3. What did the man urge everyone to do?
- (A) Tune in to the show every day
- (B) Come back and see him again
- (C) Listen to a terrific new CD
- (D) See a movie

Step 2　リーディング問題

英文を読んで、問題を解こう。＜制限時間 3 分＞

W:　Welcome to the show. It's always good to have you with us.
M:　It's my pleasure.

W:　Now, what is going on with you and Rachel Ricardo? It seems there's something about you in the press every day.
M:　OK, first of all, Rachel is a good friend. For some reason, though, people seem to think we're together.
W:　So you're saying you're not a couple at all? Then how did these rumors get started?

W:　It's been great having you on the show. Please come back and see us again.
M:　I definitely will, and everyone, do go see Heavens Above. It really is a terrific film.

Q4.　Who is the woman?
　　　(A) The man's friend　　　　(B) The hostess of a show
　　　(C) A guest on a talk show　　(D) A friend of Rachel Ricardo's

Q5.　What is true of the man and Rachel Ricardo?
　　　(A) They are a couple.
　　　(B) A lot of people have seen them together.
　　　(C) A lot is written about them in the press.
　　　(D) They recently starred in a movie together.

Q6.　What does the woman ask the man about?
　　　(A) His career　　　(B) His movie
　　　(C) His hobbies　　(D) His love life

Step 3　文法・語彙問題
空欄にふさわしい語句を選ぼう。＜制限時間2分＞

Q7. You don't need to thank me. It's my ----.
 (A) pleased
 (B) pleasurable
 (C) pleasant
 (D) pleasure

Q8. What is ---- on with you and Rachel?
 (A) going
 (B) making
 (C) doing
 (D) being

Q9. You're saying you're not a couple ----?
 (A) in all
 (B) all that
 (C) at all
 (D) all time

Q10. My question is "How did these rumors get ----- ?"
 (A) to start
 (B) starting
 (C) start
 (D) started

Q11. It seems there's ----- about you in the press all the time.
 (A) something
 (B) anything
 (C) somewhat
 (D) some

Step 4 解答・解説チェック

現時点での理解度を確認しよう。

問題文は、トーク・ショー番組での司会者とゲストの会話です。

1. 正解 **(B)**。質問:「この会話は、どこで行なわれましたか?」。答え:「テレビ局のスタジオ」。ヒント: Welcome to the show.
2. 正解 **(C)**。質問:「女性は、なぜ男性にまた会いたいのですか?」。答え:「彼は、よいゲストだから」。ヒント: It's been great having you on the show.
3. 正解 **(D)**。質問:「男性は、皆に対して、何をするよう促しましたか?」。答え:「映画を観る」。ヒント: everyone, do go see Heavens Above.
4. 正解 **(B)**。質問:「女性は、どんな人ですか?」。答え:「番組の司会」。ヒント: Welcome to the show.
5. 正解 **(C)**。質問:「男性とレイチェル・リカルドについて、正しい記述はどれですか?」。答え:「新聞に多くの記事が書かれている」。ヒント: It seems there's something about you in the press every day.
6. 正解 **(D)**。質問:「女性は、男性に何について尋ねていますか?」。答え:「彼の恋愛生活」。ヒント: what is going on with you and Rachel Ricardo?
7. 正解 **(D)**。my(形容詞・所有格)のあとにくるのは、名詞。pleasure「喜び」を選ぶ。(A)は動詞、be pleased で「(~を)喜ぶ」。(B)「楽しい」(形容詞)、(C)「楽しませる」(形容詞)。
8. 正解 **(A)**。文意から、What's going on with ~?「~の状況が、どうなっているのか?」を完成させる。
9. 正解 **(C)**。文意から、否定文を強調する at all「まったく」を選ぶ。
10. 正解 **(D)**。文意から、get started「始まる」を完成させる。
11. 正解 **(A)**。文意から、something about you「あなた方について何かしら」を完成させる。

Step 5　直読直解トレーニング

速読速聴力を高めよう。
（※日本語訳は、英語の原文の順序どおりに記してあります。）

W:　Welcome to the show. It's always good / to have you with us.
　　ようこそ、番組へ。よかったです、お招きできて。

M:　It's my pleasure.
　　こちらこそ。

W:　Now, what is going on / with you and Rachel Ricardo?
　　ところで、どうなっているのですか、あなたとレイチェル・リカルドは？
　　It seems there's something about you / in the press / every day.
　　あなたたちのことが何かしら載っているようです、新聞に、毎日。

M:　OK, first of all, Rachel is a good friend. For some reason,
　　わかりました、まず、レイチェルは仲のよい友だちです。なぜか、
　　though, people seem to think / we're together.
　　でも、人びとは思っているようです、私たちが付き合っていると。

W:　So / you're saying / you're not a couple / at all?
　　では、ということですか、2人は恋人同士ではない、まったく？
　　Then / how did these rumors get started?
　　それでは、どのようにこうした噂が始まったのでしょう？

W:　It's been great / having you on the show.
　　ありがとうございました、番組にお越しいただき。
　　Please come back / and see us again.
　　ぜひまた、いらしてください。

M:　I definitely will, and everyone, do go see Heavens Above.
　　もちろんです、そしてみなさん、ぜひ『天空の楽園』を観に行ってください。
　　It really is a terrific film.
　　本当にすばらしい映画ですよ。

語句

have：〜を招く　　press：新聞　　first of all：最初に　　for some reason：なぜか
though：けれども　　seem to：〜のようである　　together：特別な仲で　　rumor：噂
definitely：確実に　　terrific：すばらしい

Step 6　基本構文トレーニング
文法・語彙力を高めよう。

131	ようこそ、番組へ。	Welcome to the show.
132	お招きできて、よかったです。	It's always good to have you with us.
133	こちらこそ。	It's my pleasure.
134	あなたとレイチェルは、どうなっているのですか？	What is going on with you and Rachel?
135	あなたたちのことが何かしら新聞に載っているようです。	There's something about you in the press.
136	レイチェルは仲のよい友だちです。	Rachel is a good friend.
137	人びとは私たちが付き合っていると思っているようです。	People seem to think we're together.
138	2人は、まったく恋人同士ではない、ということですか？	You're saying you're not a couple at all?
139	どのようにして、こうした噂が始まったのでしょう？	How did these rumors get started?
140	番組にお越しいただき、ありがとうございました。	It's been great having you on the show.

Day 5 説明文トレーニング

Step 1 リスニング問題
CDを聞いて、問題を解こう。＜制限時間2分＞

Q1. What is the speaker holding?
- (A) Money
- (B) Papers
- (C) Food
- (D) Clothing

Q2. What is true of the speaker?
- (A) He is giving instructions.
- (B) He is sending his children to camp.
- (C) He is going to a summer camp.
- (D) He is trying to get a summer job.

Q3. What do people who sign up have to do in a week or so?
- (A) Register
- (B) Talk to the speaker in person
- (C) Pay
- (D) Go pick up their children

Step 2　リーディング問題
英文を読んで、問題を解こう。＜制限時間3分＞

Could I have your attention, please? Parents must fill in two forms if they wish to sign their children up for any of our camps. This yellow one I have in my hand here is the general registration form. You need this other form, too. It's for whatever camp you want to sign your children up for. So if you are signing up your little one for band camp or, say, adventure camp, or whatever camp, for that specific form, go to that camp's information table. Everyone got that? And don't panic about paying today. We will be sending out invoices later this week. Today is for registration only.

Q4. Who is being spoken to?
　　(A) Teachers
　　(B) Campers
　　(C) Children
　　(D) Parents

Q5. What must be done today?
　　(A) Payments must be made.
　　(B) Forms must be filled out.
　　(C) Invoices must be received.
　　(D) Children must be interviewed.

Q6. What information is given in this meeting?
　　(A) The camps are not expensive.
　　(B) There is more than one kind of camp.
　　(C) The camps will open later in the week.
　　(D) There are more than two forms for each camp.

Step 3　文法・語彙問題

空欄にふさわしい語句を選ぼう。＜制限時間 2 分＞

Q7. They wish to sign their children ------ for summer camp.
　　(A) out
　　(B) over
　　(C) down
　　(D) up

Q8. Of the two forms, this yellow one is the general ------ form.
　　(A) specific
　　(B) adventure
　　(C) attention
　　(D) registration

Q9. Don't panic about ------ today, because you can pay later.
　　(A) paying
　　(B) pay
　　(C) paid
　　(D) to pay

Q10. Parents must fill ----- two forms for each child.
　　(A) up
　　(B) in
　　(C) on
　　(D) into

Q11. We ----- out invoices later this week to everyone who registers.
　　(A) will be sent
　　(B) send
　　(C) will be sending
　　(D) sent

Step 4 解答・解説チェック
現時点での理解度を確認しよう。

問題文は、サマーキャンプへの参加の登録受付の呼びかけです。

1. 正解 **(B)**。質問：「話し手は、何を持っていますか？」。答え：「書類」。ヒント：This yellow one I have in my hand here is the general registration form.
2. 正解 **(A)**。質問：「話し手に関して、正しいものはどれですか？」。答え：「彼は、説明をしている」。ヒント：話の内容全体から。
3. 正解 **(C)**。質問：「申し込みをした人は、1, 2週間の内に何をしなければなりませんか？」。答え：「支払い」。ヒント：don't panic about paying today. We will be sending out invoices later this week.
4. 正解 **(D)**。質問：「話を聞いているのは、どんな人ですか？」。答え：「保護者（父兄）」。ヒント：Parents must fill in
5. 正解 **(B)**。質問：「今日すべきことは、何ですか？」。答え：「書類を記入する」。ヒント：fill in two forms if they wish to sign their children up, Today is for registration only.
6. 正解 **(B)**。質問：「この会合で提供される情報は、何ですか？」。答え：「2種類以上のキャンプがある」。ヒント：for any of our camps
7. 正解 **(D)**。sign +（人）+ up「（人）を申し込む」を完成させる。
8. 正解 **(D)**。文意から、registration form「登録用紙」を完成させる。(A)「特定の」は、general「一般の」と矛盾するので不可。
9. 正解 **(A)**。panic about + 動詞 ing「慌てて～する」を完成させる。
10. 正解 **(B)**。文意から、fill in「～（の空欄）に記入する」を完成させる。(A) は、「（容器などを）満たす」。
11. 正解 **(C)**。later this week「今週後半に」という文意から、近い未来の確実な行為を表わす will be sending（未来進行形）を完成させる。

Step 5　直読直解トレーニング
速読速聴力を高めよう。

Could I have your attention, please? Parents must fill in two forms /
みなさんご注目ください。ご父兄の方は、2つの用紙にご記入いただきます、
if they wish / to sign their children up / for any of our camps.
ご希望でしたら、お子様の申し込みを、私どものキャンプのいずれかに。
This yellow one / I have in my hand here / is the general registration form.
この黄色のものは、私がこの手に持っている、一般の登録用紙です。
You need this other form, too. It's for whatever camp / you want /
このもう1つの用紙も必要です。すべてのキャンプ用です、あなたが望む、
to sign your children up for. So / if you are signing up / your little one /
お子様の申し込みをしたいと。ですから、申し込みをされるなら、お子様を、
for band camp or, say, adventure camp, or whatever camp,
バンド・キャンプとか、たとえば、冒険キャンプ、あるいはどんなキャンプでも、
for that specific form, go to that camp's information table.
専用の用紙を取りに、あそこのキャンプ案内テーブルに行ってください。
Everyone got that? And don't panic / about paying today.
みなさん、おわかりですか？　そして慌てないでください、本日の支払いを。
We will be sending out invoices / later this week. Today is /
請求書をお送りします、今週のちほど。本日は、
for registration only.
登録だけです。

語句

- **parent**：保護者（父兄）
- **form**：申込用紙
- **general**：一般的な
- **whatever**：どんな～でも
- **panic**：慌てる
- **fill in**：～に記入する
- **sign up**：～を申し込む
- **registration**：登録
- **specific**：特定の
- **invoice**：請求書

Step 6　基本構文トレーニング
文法・語彙力を高めよう。

141	ご注目ください。	Could I have your attention, please?
142	ご父兄の方は、2つの用紙にご記入いただきます。	Parents must fill in two forms.
143	彼らは、子供の申し込みを希望しています。	They wish to sign their children up.
144	この黄色のものは一般の登録用紙です。	This yellow one is the general registration form.
145	この、もう1つの用紙も必要です。	You need this other form, too.
146	あそこのキャンプの案内テーブルに行ってください。	Go to that camp's information table.
147	みなさん、おわかりですか？	Everyone got that?
148	本日慌ててお支払いになる必要はありません。	Don't panic about paying today.
149	今週、のちほど請求書をお送りいたします。	We will be sending out invoices later this week.
150	本日は、登録だけです。	Today is for registration only.

Day 6 チェックテスト

ふさわしい語句の意味を選ぼう。＜制限時間5分＞

1. disagree：(A) 消える　(B) がっかりさせる　(C) 意見が合わない
2. length：(A) 長さ　(B) 笑う　(C) 脚
3. contract：(A) 接触　(B) 契約　(C) 破棄
4. clause：(A) 閉鎖　(B) 接近　(C) 条項
5. insist:：(A) 接触　(B) 要求する　(C) 破棄
6. deal：(A) 契約　(B) 条件　(C) 計算
7. uproot：(A) 根の上部　(B) 〜を引っ越しさせる　(C) 屋根を付ける
8. supervisor：(A) サンバイザー　(B) 管理者　(C) 雇用者
9. budge：(A) 意見を述べる　(B) 意見を変える　(C) 意見を否定する
10. appreciate：(A) 〜を批評する　(B) 〜に応募する　(C) 〜を感謝する

11. in particular：(A) 特に　(B) 実践的に　(C) 特殊な
12. curious about：(A) 〜に癒し効果のある　(B) 〜に不安を感じる　(C) 〜に興味がある
13. half-off：(A) 前半の　(B) 半額の　(C) 半分欠けた
14. wonder if：(A) 〜を探検する　(B) 〜かなと思う　(C) もし〜迷ったら
15. discontinue：(A) 〜を継続する　(B) 〜を中止する　(C) 〜を切り離す
16. buy out：(A) 〜を買収する　(B) 買い物に出かける　(C) 買いまくる
17. extra：(A) 新規の　(B) 最低な　(C) 余分の
18. around here：(A) この円の周り　(B) 間もなく　(C) この辺
19. somewhere：(A) 何カ所か　(B) どこか　(C) どこにでも
20. total：(A) 合計　(B) 小計　(C) 金額

21. wallet：(A) 鞄　(B) 財布　(C) 腕輪
22. available：(A) 効果がある　(B) 利用できる　(C) 価値がある

23. actually：(A) しらじらしく　(B) 演技が入って　(C) 実際に
24. go ahead：(A) 話を進める　(B) 頭から先に　(C) 1人ずつ
25. flag：(A) 〜を合図で停止させる　(B) 〜を合図で出発させる
    (C) 〜を合図で反転させる
26. charge：(A) 法律　(B) 料金　(C) 規則
27. show up：(A) 現われる　(B) 消える　(C) 立ち去る
28. replacement card：(A) 再発行カード　(B) 盗難カード　(C) 家族カード
29. send out：(A) 〜を売り切る　(B) 〜を郵送する　(C) 在庫切れになる
30. great relief：(A) 大きな彫刻　(B) 偉大な投手　(C) 大きな安堵

31. have：(A) 〜を招く　(B) 〜を作る　(C) 〜を立てる
32. press：(A) 以前の　(B) テレビ　(C) 新聞
33. first of all：(A) 最初に　(B) 全員に　(C) 大事な
34. for some reason：(A) 〜の理由で　(B) なぜか　(C) 誰かのせいで
35. though：(A) 考え　(B) しっかりと　(C) けれども
36. seem to：(A) 〜に違いない　(B) 〜のようである　(C) 〜すべきである
37. together：(A) 特別な仲で　(B) 敵対して　(C) 仲直りして
38. rumor：(A) 賃借人　(B) 想像　(C) 噂
39. definitely：(A) 確実に　(B) おそらく　(C) ひょっとすると
40. terrific：(A) 交通　(B) すばらしい　(C) ひどい

41. parent：(A) 部分　(B) 特許　(C) 保護者
42. fill in：(A) 〜で一杯の　(B) 〜に記入する　(C) 〜に割り込む
43. form：(A) 申込用紙　(B) 書物　(C) 参考資料
44. sign up：(A) 〜に合図を送る　(B) 看板を出す　(C) 〜を申し込む
45. general：(A) 気前のいい　(B) 一般的な　(C) 特別な
46. registration：(A) 移動　(B) 規制　(C) 登録
47. whatever：(A) どんな〜でも　(B) どこへ行っても　(C) 誰でも
48. specific：(A) 特定の　(B) 一般の　(C) 参考の
49. panic：(A) 慌てる　(B) ピクニック　(C) パックする
50. invoice：(A) 解説書　(B) 請求書　(C) 留守電

チェックテスト解答

1. **(C)**	2. **(A)**	3. **(B)**	4. **(C)**	5. **(B)**
6. **(A)**	7. **(B)**	8. **(B)**	9. **(B)**	10. **(C)**
11. **(A)**	12. **(C)**	13. **(B)**	14. **(B)**	15. **(B)**
16. **(A)**	17. **(C)**	18. **(C)**	19. **(B)**	20. **(A)**
21. **(B)**	22. **(B)**	23. **(C)**	24. **(A)**	25. **(A)**
26. **(B)**	27. **(A)**	28. **(A)**	29. **(B)**	30. **(C)**
31. **(A)**	32. **(C)**	33. **(A)**	34. **(B)**	35. **(C)**
36. **(B)**	37. **(A)**	38. **(C)**	39. **(A)**	40. **(B)**
41. **(C)**	42. **(B)**	43. **(A)**	44. **(C)**	45. **(B)**
46. **(C)**	47. **(A)**	48. **(A)**	49. **(A)**	50. **(B)**

＜ワンポイント＞

　第3週のトレーニングはいかがでしたか？　ナチュラルスピードのリスングに慣れてきましたか？　少し耳がなじんできた気がしたら、「リラックスして聞く」ことができ始めている証拠です。でも、耳はなじんできたけれど、「リーディングでは、知らない単語が多くて理解できない」という方も多いはずです。

　実は、リーディング上達のコツは、「知らない単語は無視すること」です。リスニングでは、知らない単語は聞き取れませんから、自然に無視しているのですが、リーディングでは、知らない単語が目に飛び込んできてしまいます。これを無視して、目を先に進めることがポイントです。

　もちろん、復習の際に、知らない単語の意味を確認するのはいいことですが、問題を解く際に気にするのは NG です。知らない単語に意識を向けるのではなく、知っている単語から想像しましょう。リスニング力同様、リーディング力も想像力です。

第 **5** 章

Week 4

Week 4
今週のトレーニング

Day 1〜 Day 5 のトレーニング			
Step		内容	時間
1		リスニング問題（3問）	2分
2		リーディング問題（3問）	3分
3		文法・語彙問題（5問）	2分
4		解答・解説チェック	3分
5	直読直解トレーニング		5〜15分
	①	CD（英語）を聞いて、英文を目で追う。	
	②	CD（英語）を聞いて、日本語訳を目で追う。	
	③	カンマ (,)、ピリオド (.)、スラッシュ (/) の単位で、英文の意味が理解できるか確認（理解できない部分は、日本語訳や語彙を参照）。	
6	基本構文トレーニング		5〜15分
	①	1文ずつCD（日本語・英語）を聞き、英語を数回音読。	
	②	10文の英語を続けて音読（数回行なう）。	
	③	テキストを縦に半分に折るなどして日本語訳を隠し、英語部分を見て意味がすぐにわかるか確認。	
	④	応用トレーニング「ルックアップ＆セイ」「音読筆写」「リピーティング」	

＜ワンポイント＞

　移動中などに、音声 CD を使って「基本構文のシャドウイング」（12ページ）を、試してみましたか？　うまくできないという方は、応用トレーニングに「リピーティング」を加えると、シャドウイングが楽になるはずです。

リピーティング	基本構文（日→英）を聞き、英語のあとで一時停止して、何も見ずに聞き取った英語を話します。

Day 1 会話文トレーニング

Step 1 リスニング問題
CDを聞いて、問題を解こう。＜制限時間2分＞

Q1. What is true of the man and woman?
　　(A) They just met.
　　(B) They went to school together.
　　(C) They work together.
　　(D) They are childhood friends.

Q2. What are the two people talking about?
　　(A) Their dreams
　　(B) Their jobs
　　(C) Their families
　　(D) Their hobbies

Q3. Where does the man live?
　　(A) In Kansas City
　　(B) In Odessa
　　(C) In St. Paul
　　(D) In San Francisco

Step 2　リーディング問題

英文を読んで、問題を解こう。＜制限時間3分＞

W: Hi, Paul. I'm Julie.

M: Hi, Julie. Actually, it's Paulo. They spelled my name wrong on the name tag.

W: When did you move to San Francisco, Paulo?

M: When I got the job with Odessa Systems. And you work in the Kansas City distribution center?

W: No, I work out of Kansas City. I'm on the road virtually three weeks every month.

W: Anyway, Paulo. Let me give you my card. I do get to San Francisco almost every month.

M: Great. Here's my card, too. E-mail is the best way to get in touch with me. Next time you're here, let me be your guide.

Q4. Where does this conversation take place?
　　(A) In Odessa　　　　　　(B) In São Paulo
　　(C) In Kansas City　　　　(D) In San Francisco

Q5. What is true of Julie?
　　(A) She lives in Kansas City.
　　(B) She was born in Kansas City.
　　(C) She invites Paulo to Kansas City.
　　(D) She mostly works out of Kansas City.

Q6. What does Paulo invite Julie to do?
　　(A) Have dinner　　　　　　(B) Contact him later
　　(C) Go to San Francisco　　(D) Work for Odessa Systems

Step 3　文法・語彙問題

空欄にふさわしい語句を選ぼう。＜制限時間 2 分＞

Q7. I'm sorry, but they spelled my name ----- on the name tag.
　　(A) bad
　　(B) mistake
　　(C) error
　　(D) wrong

Q8. I ----- the job with Odessa Systems about a year ago.
　　(A) was hired
　　(B) was found
　　(C) got
　　(D) made

Q9. You work in the Kansas City ----- center, don't you?
　　(A) distribute
　　(B) distribution
　　(C) distributed
　　(D) distributes

Q10. I'm ----- the road virtually three weeks every month.
　　(A) on
　　(B) in
　　(C) to
　　(D) for

Q11. Next time you're here, ----- me be your guide.
　　(A) leave
　　(B) let
　　(C) make
　　(D) ask

Step 4　解答・解説チェック

現時点での理解度を確認しよう。

問題文は、コンベンションで知り合った男女の会話です。

1. 正解 **(A)**。質問:「男性と女性について、正しい記述は何ですか」。答え:「出会ったばかり」。ヒント:Hi, Paul. I'm Julie.
2. 正解 **(B)**。質問:「2人は、何について話していますか?」。答え:「彼らの仕事」。ヒント:you work in the Kansas City distribution center?, I work out of Kansas City. など。
3. 正解 **(D)**。質問:「男性は、どこに住んでいますか?」。答え:「サンフランシスコ」。ヒント:When did you move to San Francisco, Paulo?
4. 正解 **(D)**。質問:「この会話は、どこで行なわれていますか?」。答え:「サンフランシスコで」。ヒント:When did you move to San Francisco, Paulo?, Next time you're here, let me be your guide.
5. 正解 **(D)**。質問:「ジュリーに関して、正しい記述はどれですか?」。答え:「彼女は、ほとんどカンザスシティの外で働いている」。ヒント:I work out of Kansas City. I'm on the road virtually three weeks every month.
6. 正解 **(B)**。質問:「パウロは、ジュリーに何をするよう勧めましたか?」。答え:「あとで連絡するように」。ヒント:Here's my card, too. E-mail is the best way to get in touch with me.
7. 正解 **(D)**。spell one's name wrong「(人)の名前のつづりを間違える」の過去形を完成させる。
8. 正解 **(C)**。get the job with「~に就職する」の過去形を完成させる。
9. 正解 **(B)**。distribution center「配送センター」を完成させる。
10. 正解 **(A)**。on the road「(出張などで)旅に出ている」を完成させる。
11. 正解 **(B)**。let me + 動詞「私に~させてください」を完成させる。

Step 5　直読直解トレーニング

速読速聴力を高めよう。
(※日本語訳は、英語の原文の順序どおりに記してあります。)

W:　Hi, Paul. I'm Julie.
　　こんにちは、ポール。ジュリーです。

M:　Hi, Julie. Actually, it's Paulo.
　　こんにちは、ジュリー。実は、パウロです。
　　They spelled my name wrong / on the name tag.
　　彼らが私の名前のつづりを間違えたのです、名札の。

W:　When did you move / to San Francisco, Paulo?
　　いつ引っ越したのですか、サンフランシスコに、パウロ？

M:　When I got the job / with Odessa Systems.
　　就職した時です、オデッサ・システムズに。
　　And you work / in the Kansas City distribution center?
　　そして、あなたは勤めているのですね、カンザスシティの配送センターで？

W:　No, I work out of Kansas City.
　　いいえ、カンザスシティの外で働いています。
　　I'm on the road / virtually three weeks every month.
　　出張に出ています、毎月ほとんど3週間は。

W:　Anyway, Paulo. Let me give you my card.
　　いずれにしても、パウロ。名刺をお渡しします。
　　I do get to San Francisco / almost every month.
　　サンフランシスコに来ます、ほぼ毎月。

M:　Great. Here's my card, too. E-mail is the best way / to get in touch
　　それは結構。私の名刺です。Eメールがいちばんです、私と連絡を取るには。
　　with me. Next time you're here, let me be your guide.
　　今度あなたがここに来る時は、私がガイドをします。

語句
spell：〜をつづる　**name tag**：名札　**distribution**：配送　**out of**：〜から外へ
on the road：出張中　**virtually**：ほとんど　**get to**：〜に到着する　**here's**：これが〜です
best way：最良の方法　**get in touch with**：〜と連絡を取る

Step 6 基本構文トレーニング
文法・語彙力を高めよう。

151	彼らは、名札の私の名前のつづりを間違えました。	They spelled my name wrong on the name tag.
152	いつサンフランシスコに引っ越したのですか？	When did you move to San Francisco?
153	オデッサ・システムズに就職しました。	I got the job with Odessa Systems.
154	あなたは、カンザスシティの配送センターに勤めているのですね？	You work in the Kansas City distribution center?
155	カンザスシティの外で働いています。	I work out of Kansas City.
156	毎月ほとんど3週間は出張に出ています。	I'm on the road virtually three weeks every month.
157	名刺をお渡しします。	Let me give you my card.
158	サンフランシスコには、ほぼ毎月来ます。	I do get to San Francisco almost every month.
159	連絡を取るには、Eメールがいちばんです。	E-mail is the best way to get in touch.
160	今度あなたがここに来る時は、私がガイドします。	Next time you're here, let me be your guide.

Week 4

Day 2 会話文トレーニング

Step 1 リスニング問題

CDを聞いて、問題を解こう。＜制限時間2分＞

Q1. What are the people looking at?
 (A) A newspaper
 (B) A television
 (C) A menu
 (D) A map

Q2. What are the people talking about?
 (A) Sports
 (B) The weekend
 (C) The weather
 (D) Politics

Q3. What is the woman worried about?
 (A) Losing her job
 (B) Getting wet
 (C) Being late for an appointment
 (D) Having an accident

Step 2　リーディング問題
英文を読んで、問題を解こう。＜制限時間3分＞

W: Honey, could you flip over to the weather channel and check the forecast for today? I hope I don't need my umbrella again today.
M: OK . . . Looks like it'll be cloudy with light showers in the afternoon.

W: So I'd better take my umbrella then, I guess. Better safe than sorry.
M: I think you can risk it. Look at the clouds out there—hardly any at all.
W: Even so, I'd rather not take a chance.

W: Did they run the long-range forecast yet? I want to know about the weekend.
M: It says it's coming up in five minutes.

Q4. What does the woman ask the man to do?
　(A) Turn on the television
　(B) Bring her umbrella to her
　(C) Call the weather service
　(D) Check the weather forecast

Q5. What does the woman decide?
　(A) To take her umbrella
　(B) To wear a raincoat
　(C) To take a chance
　(D) To look at the clouds

Q6. What will happen in five minutes?
　(A) The woman will leave for work.
　(B) The weekend weather will be reported.
　(C) There will be light showers.
　(D) The man will turn off the television.

Step 3　文法・語彙問題

空欄にふさわしい語句を選ぼう。＜制限時間２分＞

Q7. ----- you flip over to the weather channel for a minute?
（A）Could
（B）Please
（C）Shall
（D）Request

Q8. It'll be cloudy with light ----- in the afternoon.
（A）showers
（B）storms
（C）waters
（D）hurricanes

Q9. I'd better ----- my umbrella in case it rains.
（A）taken
（B）taking
（C）to take
（D）take

Q10. As they say, "Better safe than -----."
（A）you're sorry
（B）sorry
（C）danger
（D）you're unsafe

Q11. I think you can ----- it without an umbrella.
（A）luck
（B）gamble
（C）risk
（D）no trouble

Step 4　解答・解説チェック

現時点での理解度を確認しよう。

問題文は、天気予報について話す男女の会話です。

1. 正解 **(B)**。質問：「話し手たちは、何を見ていますか？」。答え：「テレビ」。ヒント：could you flip over to the weather channel
2. 正解 **(C)**。質問：「話し手たちは、何について話していますか？」。答え：「天気」。ヒント：I'd better take my umbrella, Looks like it'll be cloudy
3. 正解 **(B)**。質問：「女性は、何を心配していますか？」。答え：「濡れること」。ヒント：I'd better take my umbrella, then.
4. 正解 **(D)**。質問：「女性は、男性に何をするよう頼んでいますか？」。答え：「天気予報を調べる」。ヒント：could you flip over to the weather channel and check the forecast
5. 正解 **(A)**。質問：「女性は、どうすることに決めましたか？」。答え：「傘を持っていく」。ヒント：I'd better take my umbrella
6. 正解 **(B)**。質問：「5分後に何が起こりますか？」。答え：「週末の天気予報が放送される」。ヒント：It says it's coming up in five minutes.
7. 正解 **(A)**。Could you + 動詞？「〜していただけますか？」を完成させる。
8. 正解 **(A)**。light showers「弱いにわか雨」を完成させる。
9. 正解 **(D)**。take を選び、I'd better + 動詞（原形）「〜したほうがよい」を完成させる。
10. 正解 **(B)**。Better safe than sorry.「用心に越したことはない」を完成させる。
11. 正解 **(C)**。risk it「リスクを冒してやってみる」を完成させる。

Step 5　直読直解トレーニング

速読速聴力を高めよう。

（※日本語訳は、英語の原文の順序どおりに記してあります。）

W:　Honey, could you flip over / to the weather channel /
　　あなた、切り替えて、天気チャンネルに、
　　and check the forecast / for today?
　　そして天気予報をチェックしてくれますか、今日の？
　　I hope / I don't need my umbrella again today.
　　望みます、今日も傘がいらないことを。

M:　OK... / Looks like it'll be cloudy / with light showers / in the afternoon.
　　えーと……曇りのようです、小雨が降って、午後には。

W:　So / I'd better take my umbrella then, I guess. Better safe than sorry.
　　では、傘を持っていったほうがよさそうね。用心に越したことはありません。

M:　I think / you can risk it.
　　思います、持たずに行ってもいいと。
　　Look at the clouds out there — / hardly any at all.
　　向こうの雲を見てください、ほとんどありません。

W:　Even so, I'd rather not take a chance.
　　そうだとしても、危険は冒したくありません。

W:　Did they run the long-range forecast yet?
　　長期予報はもう放送されましたか？
　　I want to know / about the weekend.
　　知りたいです、週末の予報を。

M:　It says / it's coming up / in five minutes.
　　言っています、それは始まると、5分後に。

語句　flip over：チャンネルを変える　　weather：天候　　forecast：天気予報
　　cloudy：曇り　　shower：にわか雨　　sorry：残念な　　risk it：危険を冒す
　　take a chance：一か八かやってみる　　long-range：長期の　　come up：やって来る

Step 6　基本構文トレーニング

文法・語彙力を高めよう。

161	天気チャンネルに切り替えてくれますか？	Could you flip over to the weather channel?
162	今日の天気予報をチェックしてください。	Check the forecast for today.
163	曇りで、午後には小雨が降るでしょう。	It'll be cloudy with light showers in the afternoon.
164	傘を持っていったほうがよさそうです。	I'd better take my umbrella.
165	用心に越したことはありません。	Better safe than sorry.
166	あえてしてみてもいいと思います。	I think you can risk it.
167	危険は冒したくありません。	I'd rather not take a chance.
168	長期予報はもう放送されましたか？	Did they run the long-range forecast yet?
169	週末の予報を知りたいです。	I want to know about the weekend.
170	それは、5分後に始まると言っています。	It says it's coming up in five minutes.

Day 3 会話文トレーニング

Step 1 リスニング問題
CDを聞いて、問題を解こう。＜制限時間2分＞

Q1. How did the weather seem when the people were talking?
　　(A) Too hot to do any work
　　(B) Snowing
　　(C) Rainy
　　(D) Fine

Q2. What have the speakers been doing?
　　(A) Working outside
　　(B) Moving a fence
　　(C) Preparing a meal
　　(D) Working in an office

Q3. What are the speakers going to do next?
　　(A) Get on a train
　　(B) Eat
　　(C) Sleep
　　(D) Go to work

Step 2　リーディング問題

英文を読んで、問題を解こう。＜制限時間 3 分＞

W: I'm done with mowing the lawn. Do you need any help with the garden?
M: Well, could you prune the rose bushes? You're much better at that than I am.

W: Done. Want me to fix us some lunch?
M: Sounds good. I'll be done here with the hedges in about ten minutes.
W: OK. Does some leftover pasta and some of that minestrone soup sound good?

W: We really should think about fixing the back fence, too.
M: I'm already on that. I've ordered some new slats. They should be delivered on Friday.

Q4. When the dialogue begins, what has the woman been doing?
　　(A) Trimming the rose bushes
　　(B) Fixing some lunch
　　(C) Cutting the grass
　　(D) Working on the hedges

Q5. Where are these people?
　　(A) In their own garden
　　(B) In someone else's yard
　　(C) In their kitchen
　　(D) In a garden-supply store

Q6. How will the Friday delivery be used?
　　(A) To prune the rose bushes　　(B) To repair the fence
　　(C) To mow the lawn　　(D) To trim the hedges

Step 3　文法・語彙問題

空欄にふさわしい語句を選ぼう。＜制限時間2分＞

Q7. I'm ----- with mowing the lawn, so what can I do next?
（A）gone
（B）made
（C）run
（D）done

Q8. I've finished the front, so do you need ----- help with the garden?
（A）to
（B）something
（C）any
（D）anything

Q9. Thanks for your help, because you're much better ----- that than I am.
（A）at
（B）to
（C）of
（D）by

Q10. We really should think about ----- the back fence.
（A）fixed
（B）fixing
（C）to fix
（D）fix

Q11. They should ----- delivered on Friday, the garden shop said.
（A）be
（B）been
（C）being
（D）to be

Step 4　解答・解説チェック

現時点での理解度を確認しよう。

問題文は、庭の手入れをしている男女の会話です。

1. 正解 **(D)**。質問：「話し手たちが話している時の天気は、どうでしたか？」。答え：「晴れ」。ヒント：I'm done with mowing the lawn.
2. 正解 **(A)**。質問：「話し手たちは、何をしていましたか？」。答え：「外での作業」。ヒント：前半の会話の内容から、外で作業をしていることがわかる。
3. 正解 **(B)**。質問：「話し手たちは、次に何をしますか？」。答え：「食事」。ヒント：Want me to fix us some lunch?
4. 正解 **(C)**。質問：「会話が始まった時、女性は何をしていましたか？」。答え：「草刈りをしていた」。ヒント：I'm done with mowing the lawn.
5. 正解 **(A)**。質問：「話し手たちは、どこにいますか？」。答え：「自分たちの家の庭」。ヒント：庭の話と、ランチを作る話から。
6. 正解 **(B)**。質問：「金曜日に配達されるものは、何に使われますか？」。答え：「フェンスを修理するために」。ヒント：最後の2行のやり取り。
7. 正解 **(D)**。be done with + 名詞相当語句「～が終了した」を完成させる。
8. 正解 **(C)**。do you need any help with ～？「～に何か手伝いが必要か？」を完成させる。（A）は、「あなたが手伝う必要があるか？」で文意にあわない。
9. 正解 **(A)**。文意から、be good at「～がうまい」の比較級を完成させる。
10. 正解 **(B)**。fixing を選び、think about + 動詞 ing「～について考える」を完成させる。
11. 正解 **(A)**。「配達される」という文意から、be delivered（受動態）を完成させる。

Week 4

Step 5　直読直解トレーニング
速読速聴力を高めよう。
(※日本語訳は、英語の原文の順序どおりに記してあります。)

W: I'm done / with mowing the lawn.
　　終わりました、芝刈りは。
　　Do you need any help / with the garden?
　　何か手伝いが必要ですか、庭で？

M: Well, could you prune the rose bushes?
　　そうですね、バラの植え込みを刈り込んでくれますか？
　　You're much better at that / than I am.
　　それはあなたのほうがずっと上手です、私より。

W: Done. Want me to fix us some lunch?
　　終わりました。何かランチを作りましょうか？

M: Sounds good. I'll be done here / with the hedges /
　　いいですね。ここが終わります、生け垣が、
　　in about ten minutes.
　　あと10分ぐらいで。

W: OK. Does some leftover pasta / and some of that minestrone soup /
　　わかりました。パスタの残りと、あのミネストローネスープで、
　　sound good?
　　いいですか？

W: We really should think / about fixing the back fence, too.
　　私たちは、本当に考えないといけません、裏のフェンスの修理についても。

M: I'm already on that. I've ordered some new slats.
　　それについて、すでに考えています。新しい薄板を注文しました。
　　They should be delivered / on Friday.
　　それらは、配達されるはずです、金曜日に。

語句
mow：〜を刈り取る　lawn：芝　prune：〜を刈り込む　bush：茂み
fix：〜を料理する　hedge：生け垣　leftover：残りの　fix：〜を修理する
slat：薄板　deliver：〜を配達する

Step 6　基本構文トレーニング
文法・語彙力を高めよう。

171	芝刈りは、終わりました。	I'm done with mowing the lawn.
172	庭で、何か手伝いが必要ですか？	Do you need any help with the garden?
173	バラの植え込みを刈り込んでくれますか？	Could you prune the rose bushes?
174	それについては、あなたのほうが私よりもずっと上手です。	You're much better at that than I am.
175	何かランチを作りましょうか？	Want me to fix us some lunch?
176	パスタの残りで、いいですか？	Does some leftover pasta sound good?
177	私たちは、裏のフェンスの修理について、本当に考えないといけません。	We really should think about fixing the back fence.
178	それについて、すでに考えています。	I'm already on that.
179	新しい薄板を注文しました。	I've ordered some new slats.
180	それらは、金曜日に配達されるはずです。	They should be delivered on Friday.

Day 4　会話文トレーニング

Step 1　リスニング問題
CDを聞いて、問題を解こう。＜制限時間2分＞

Q1. Where is Ray going?
   (A) To a bank
   (B) To work
   (C) To school
   (D) To a hospital

Q2. What did the woman think of Ray's news?
   (A) She was surprised.
   (B) She was disappointed.
   (C) It angered her.
   (D) It confused her.

Q3. When did the conversation take place?
   (A) In the early morning
   (B) At noon
   (C) In the early evening
   (D) At midnight

Step 2　リーディング問題
英文を読んで、問題を解こう。＜制限時間３分＞

W: Where are you off to in such a hurry there, Ray?
M: I have to get to my computer class. I'm running a little late.

W: I had no idea you were taking a night course. How is it?
M: It's great. I'm learning a lot. My teacher explains things in a really simple way.
W: I should look into improving my skills, too.

W: So would you recommend this school?
M: Without a doubt. Their tuition fees are reasonable, too.

Q4. At the start of the dialogue, why does the woman ask the man a question?
　　(A) Because he is running.
　　(B) Because he is studying.
　　(C) Because he is leaving quickly.
　　(D) Because he is looking at a computer.

Q5. What did the woman not know until now?
　　(A) That the man is taking a class.
　　(B) That night courses are available.
　　(C) That using a computer is simple.
　　(D) That her skills need to be improved.

Q6. What is the man's opinion of the school?
　　(A) He thinks it is good.
　　(B) He could not recommend it.
　　(C) He has some doubts about it.
　　(D) He likes it although the fees are high.

Step 3　文法・語彙問題

空欄にふさわしい語句を選ぼう。＜制限時間2分＞

Q7. I'm ----- a little late, so I have to hurry.
（A）doing
（B）trying
（C）running
（D）standing

Q8. I'm surprised because I had ----- idea you were taking a night course.
（A）no
（B）not
（C）nothing
（D）none

Q9. My teacher explains things ----- a really simple way.
（A）of
（B）in
（C）at
（D）on

Q10. I should look into ----- my skills, too, to get a better job.
（A）improve
（B）improving
（C）to improve
（D）improvement

Q11. The teachers are good and their ----- fees are reasonable, too.
（A）celebration
（B）recommendation
（C）explanation
（D）tuition

Step 4　解答・解説チェック

現時点での理解度を確認しよう。

問題文は、コンピュータの講習に関する男女の会話です。

1. 正解 **(C)**。質問：「レイは、どこに行こうとしていますか？」。答え：「学校」。ヒント：I have to get to my computer class.
2. 正解 **(A)**。質問：「女性は、レイのニュースについてどう思いましたか？」。答え：「驚いた」。ヒント：I had no idea you were taking a night course.
3. 正解 **(C)**。質問：「この会話は、いつ行なわれましたか？」。答え：「夕方」。ヒント：Where are you off to in such a hurry there, Ray?, I had no idea you were taking a night course.
4. 正解 **(C)**。質問：「会話の最初で、女性はなぜ男性に質問したのですか？」。答え：「急いで出かけようとしていたので」。ヒント：Where are you off to in such a hurry ...?
5. 正解 **(A)**。質問：「今現在まで女性が知らなかったことは、何ですか？」。答え：「男性が授業を取っていること」。ヒント：I had no idea you were taking a night course.
6. 正解 **(A)**。質問：「学校についての男性の意見は、どうですか？」。答え：「よいと思っている」。ヒント：So would you recommend this school?, Without a doubt.
7. 正解 **(C)**。be running (a little) late「(少し) 遅れている」を完成させる。
8. 正解 **(A)**。have no idea + 節「～を知らない」の過去形を完成させる。
9. 正解 **(B)**。文意から、「手段」を意味する前置詞 in を選び、in a (really) simple way「(とても) わかりやすい方法で」を完成させる。
10. 正解 **(B)**。look into「～を検討する」の目的語（「～」の部分）が必要なので、動名詞 improving「～を進歩させること」を選ぶ。(D) は、improvement of なら可。
11. 正解 **(D)**。文意から、tuition fees「授業料」（複数形）を完成させる。

Week 4

Step 5　直読直解トレーニング
速読速聴力を高めよう。

W:　Where are you off to / in such a hurry there, Ray?
　　どこへ行くのですか、そんなに急いで、レイ？
M:　I have to get to / my computer class. I'm running a little late.
　　行かなければなりません、コンピュータの講習に。少し遅れそうです。

W:　I had no idea / you were taking a night course. How is it?
　　知りませんでした、夜間コースを取っていたなんて。どんな様子ですか？
M:　It's great. I'm learning a lot.
　　すばらしいです。ずいぶん勉強になっています。
　　My teacher explains things / in a really simple way.
　　先生は物事を説明します、とてもわかりやすく。
W:　I should look into / improving my skills, too.
　　私は考えないといけません、スキルアップを、同様に。

W:　So / would you recommend / this school?
　　では、お勧めですか、この学校は？
M:　Without a doubt. Their tuition fees are reasonable, too.
　　間違いありません。授業料がリーズナブルです、しかも。

語句		
be off to：〜へ出かける		**in such a hurry**：そんなに急いで
be running late：遅れている		**night course**：夜間コース
explain：〜を説明する		**look into**：〜を検討する
improve：〜を向上させる		**recommend**：〜を推薦する
tuition fees：授業料		**reasonable**：納得のいく

Step 6　基本構文トレーニング
文法・語彙力を高めよう。

181	そんなに急いでどこへ行くのですか？	Where are you off to in such a hurry?
182	コンピュータの講習に行かなければなりません。	I have to get to my computer class.
183	少し遅れそうです。	I'm running a little late.
184	あなたが夜間コースを取っていたなんて、知りませんでした。	I had no idea you were taking a night course.
185	どんな様子ですか？	How is it?
186	ずいぶん勉強になっています。	I'm learning a lot.
187	私の先生は、物事をとてもわかりやすく説明します。	My teacher explains things in a really simple way.
188	私も、もっとスキルアップを考えないといけません。	I should look into improving my skills, too.
189	この学校は、お勧めですか？	Would you recommend this school?
190	彼らの授業料は手頃です。	Their tuition fees are reasonable.

Week 4

Day 5　説明文トレーニング

Step 1　リスニング問題
CDを聞いて、問題を解こう。＜制限時間2分＞

Q1. Where is the speaker?
　　(A) On a train
　　(B) In a car
　　(C) In an elevator
　　(D) On a school bus

Q2. Who is the speaker talking to?
　　(A) A close friend
　　(B) A teacher
　　(C) A policeman
　　(D) A student

Q3. What will they soon pass by?
　　(A) A shopping center
　　(B) A hospital
　　(C) A school
　　(D) A movie theater

Step 2　リーディング問題

英文を読んで、問題を解こう。＜制限時間３分＞

Now, up here is a four-way stop. I want you to remember to come to a full stop. Let's not have any of those rolling stops like we had last week. That's good. Now, up ahead, you can see it's a school zone. Not only do you have to slow down and strictly obey the speed limit here, you have to watch out for those speed bumps. Throughout this area they've installed speed bumps in school zones. It's just for added safety, not to ruin the undercarriage of your vehicle. Got that? I have so many students complain about these speed bumps, but they're here for a very good reason.

Q4.　What did the student do during last week's lesson?
　　(A) Drive too fast
　　(B) Stop in a school zone
　　(C) Not fasten the seat belt soon enough
　　(D) Not stop completely at a four-way stop

Q5.　Where are the instructor and the student?
　　(A) On a public street
　　(B) On an expressway
　　(C) At a driving school
　　(D) On a school's playing field

Q6.　What does the instructor NOT say about speed bumps?
　　(A) They create safer conditions.
　　(B) They can damage the bottom of a car.
　　(C) They have been installed near schools.
　　(D) They are unnecessary and troublesome.

Step 3　文法・語彙問題

空欄にふさわしい語句を選ぼう。＜制限時間２分＞

Q7. Let's not have ----- those rolling stops the way you did last week.
　　(A) any of
　　(B) any
　　(C) anything
　　(D) anything of

Q8. You have to watch ----- those speed bumps.
　　(A) for out
　　(B) out for
　　(C) for it
　　(D) out of

Q9. They're here for a very good ----- : to make you slow down.
　　(A) plan
　　(B) aim
　　(C) reason
　　(D) idea

Q10. I want you to remember to come to a ----- stop, not just slow down.
　　(A) full
　　(B) fuller
　　(C) fullest
　　(D) fully

Q11. You have to strictly obey the ----- here, or you will be arrested.
　　(A) limit speed
　　(B) limited speed
　　(C) speed limit
　　(D) limiting speed

Step 4　解答・解説チェック

現時点での理解度を確認しよう。

問題文は、車の路上教習の様子です。

1. 正解 **(B)**。質問:「話し手は、どこにいますか?」。答え:「車の中」。ヒント:話の内容全体から車の路上教習をしていることがわかる。
2. 正解 **(D)**。質問:「話し手は、誰に話しかけていますか?」。答え:「練習生」。ヒント:I want you to remember to come to a full stop., That's good.
3. 正解 **(C)**。質問:「彼らは、間もなくどこを通過しますか?」。答え:「学校」。ヒント:Now, up ahead, you can see it's a school zone.
4. 正解 **(D)**。質問:「練習生は、先週のレッスンで何をしましたか?」。答え:「四方向一時停止で、完全に停止しなかった」。ヒント:Let's not have any of those rolling stops like we had last week.
5. 正解 **(A)**。質問:「教官と練習生は、どこにいますか?」。答え:「公道上」。ヒント:speed bumps、school zones
6. 正解 **(D)**。質問:「スピード・バンプについて、教官が言わなかったことは、何ですか?」。答え:「それらは不要で、煩わしい」。ヒント:they're here for a very good reason
7. 正解 **(A)**。文意から、否定文で、「~のうちの何も」を表わす any of を選ぶ。(B)(C)(D)の語順はない。
8. 正解 **(B)**。watch out for「~に注意する」を完成させる。
9. 正解 **(C)**。for「(理由)のために」という文意から、reason「理由」を選ぶ。(A)「計画」、(B)「目的」、(D)「考え」。
10. 正解 **(A)**。冠詞 a があるので stop は名詞。空欄には名詞を修飾する full (形容詞)がくる。
11. 正解 **(C)**。文意から、speed limit「制限速度」を選ぶ。

Step 5　直読直解トレーニング
速読速聴力を高めよう。

Now, up here is a four-way stop. I want you to remember /
さて、ここは四方向一時停止です。覚えておいてほしいのです、
to come to a full stop. Let's not have any of those rolling stops /
完全停止することを。だらだらとした停止はやめましょう、
like we had last week. That's good. Now, up ahead, you can see /
先週やったような。その調子です。さて、この先、わかりますね、
it's a school zone. Not only do you have to slow down /
スクール・ゾーンです。スピードを落とさなくてはならないだけでなく、
and strictly obey the speed limit / here, you have to watch out /
制限速度を厳守しなければなりません、ここでは、気を付けてください、
for those speed bumps. Throughout this area / they've installed /
あれらのスピード・バンプにも。この地域全体で、設けています
speed bumps / in school zones. It's just for added safety,
スピード・バンプを、通学路に。それは、より確実な安全のためで、
not to ruin the undercarriage / of your vehicle. Got that?
車台を傷めるためではありません、あなたの車両の。おわかりですか？
I have so many students / complain about these speed bumps,
生徒がたくさんいます、スピード・ハンプに苦情を述べる、
but they're here / for a very good reason.
でも、それらはここにあるのです、十分な理由があって。

語句

four-way stop：四方向一時停止	**full stop**：完全な停車
rolling stop：だらだらとした停車	**strictly**：厳格に
obey：〜に従う	
speed bump：スピード・バンプ［車を徐行させるための路面の凸凹］	
install：〜を設置する	**ruin**：〜をだめにする
vehicle：車両	**complain**：不平を言う

Step 6　基本構文トレーニング
文法・語彙力を高めよう。

191	さて、ここは四方向一時停止です。	Now, up here is a four-way stop.
192	完全停止することを覚えておいてほしいのです。	I want you to remember to come to a full stop.
193	だらだらとした停止はやめましょう。	Let's not have any of those rolling stops.
194	この先、スクール・ゾーンであることがわかりますね。	Up ahead, you can see it's a school zone.
195	スピードを落とさなければならないだけではありません。	Not only do you have to slow down.
196	制限速度を厳守しなければなりません。	You have to strictly obey the speed limit.
197	あれらのスピード・バンプに気を付けなければいけません。	You have to watch out for those speed bumps.
198	それは、より確実な安全のためです。	It's just for added safety.
199	あなたの車両の車台を傷めるためではありません。	It's not to ruin the undercarriage of your vehicle.
200	それらは、十分な理由があって、ここにあるのです。	They're here for a very good reason.

Day 6 チェックテスト

ふさわしい語句の意味を選ぼう。＜制限時間５分＞

1. spell：(A) 〜を描く　(B) 〜をつづる　(C) 〜を歌う
2. name tag：(A) 礼儀　(B) 名札　(C) 札束
3. distribution：(A) 注文　(B) 予約　(C) 配送
4. out of：(A) 〜から外へ　(B) 〜を失敗して　(C) 〜に向かう
5. on the road：(A) 野宿　(B) 工事中　(C) 出張中
6. virtually：(A) 儀礼的に　(B) ほとんど　(C) 大量に
7. get to：(A) 〜に到着する　(B) 〜を手にする　(C) 〜に乗る
8. here's：(A) これが〜です　(B) ここは〜です　(C) 〜が向こうにあります
9. best way：(A) 道案内　(B) 高速道路　(C) 最良の方法
10. get in touch with：(A) 〜に電話する　(B) 〜と連絡を取る　(C) 〜と会う

11. flip over：(A) チャンネルを変える　(B) 指を鳴らす
    (C) フリップをめくる
12. weather：(A) 〜かどうか　(B) 方向　(C) 天候
13. forecast：(A) 前進　(B) 天気予報　(C) 交通情報
14. cloudy：(A) 曇り　(B) 混雑した　(C) 誇りに満ちた
15. shower：(A) 土砂降り　(B) にわか雨　(C) 雷雨
16. sorry：(A) 残念な　(B) ありえない　(C) 困難な
17. risk it：(A) 危険を冒す　(B) 手に入れる　(C) どかす
18. take a chance：(A) 変えてみる　(B) 一か八かやってみる　(C) 偶然起こる
19. long-range：(A) 長方形の　(B) 広角の　(C) 長期の
20. come up：(A) 消えていく　(B) やって来る　(C) 正気に戻る

21. mow：(A) 〜を刈り取る　(B) 〜に餌をやる　(C) 〜に肥料をやる
22. lawn：(A) ローン　(B) 芝　(C) 生の
23. prune：(A) 〜を絞る　(B) 〜を刈り込む　(C) 〜を磨く
24. bush：(A) 芝生　(B) 牧草地　(C) 茂み

25. fix：(A) ファクスする　(B) キツネ　(C) 〜を料理する
26. hedge：(A) 生け垣　(B) 鉢植え　(C) 田んぼ
27. leftover：(A) 残りの　(B) 左手奥に　(C) 左上方に
28. fix：(A) 〜を修理する　(B) 料理　(C) 改善
29. slat：(A) 角材　(B) 薄板　(C) 丸太
30. deliver：(A) 〜を受領する　(B) 〜を配達する　(C) 〜を暴露する

31. be off to：(A) 〜に気づく　(B) 〜を求める　(C) 〜へ出かける
32. in such a hurry：(A) そんなに急いで　(B) たくさん運んで
　　　　　　　　　(C) 急いで中に入る
33. be running late：(A) 遅くまで営業している　(B) 遅れている
　　　　　　　　　(C) 渋滞している
34. night course：(A) 夜道　(B) 夜間コース　(C) 夜回り
35. explain：(A) 〜を計算する　(B) 〜を生み出す　(C) 〜を説明する
36. look into：(A) 〜を検討する　(B) 見積もる　(C) 接眼して見る
37. improve：(A) 〜に含める　(B) 〜を向上させる　(C) 〜を克服する
38. recommend：(A) 〜を思い出す　(B) 〜を推薦する　(C) 〜を批評する
39. tuition fees：(A) 視聴料　(B) 利用料　(C) 授業料
40. reasonable：(A) 納得のいく　(B) 理屈っぽい　(C) 値段の安い

41. four-way stop：(A) 4回停止　(B) 四方向一時停止　(C) 4種類の停まり方
42. full stop：(A) 渋滞　(B) 急停車　(C) 完全な停車
43. rolling stop：(A) だらだらとした停車　(B) 丸い屋根のバス停
　　　　　　　(C) 最徐行
44. strictly：(A) 厳格に　(B) まっすぐに　(C) 穏やかに
45. obey：(A) 〜に逆らう　(B) 〜に従う　(C) 〜を支払う
46. speed bump：(A) 高速での衝突　(B) 高速走行での振動
　　　　　　　(C) スピード・バンプ
47. install：(A) 〜を引き出す　(B) 〜を設置する　(C) 〜を操作する
48. ruin：(A) 〜をだめにする　(B) 〜を脅かす　(C) 〜を再開する
49. vehicle：(A) 歩行者　(B) ビル　(C) 車両
50. complain：(A) 説明する　(B) 比較する　(C) 不平を言う

チェックテスト解答

1. **(B)**	2. **(B)**	3. **(C)**	4. **(A)**	5. **(C)**
6. **(B)**	7. **(A)**	8. **(A)**	9. **(C)**	10. **(B)**
11. **(A)**	12. **(C)**	13. **(B)**	14. **(A)**	15. **(B)**
16. **(A)**	17. **(A)**	18. **(B)**	19. **(C)**	20. **(B)**
21. **(A)**	22. **(B)**	23. **(B)**	24. **(C)**	25. **(C)**
26. **(A)**	27. **(A)**	28. **(A)**	29. **(B)**	30. **(B)**
31. **(C)**	32. **(A)**	33. **(B)**	34. **(B)**	35. **(C)**
36. **(A)**	37. **(B)**	38. **(B)**	39. **(C)**	40. **(A)**
41. **(B)**	42. **(C)**	43. **(A)**	44. **(A)**	45. **(B)**
46. **(C)**	47. **(B)**	48. **(A)**	49. **(C)**	50. **(C)**

＜ワンポイント＞

　第4週のトレーニング、お疲れさまでした。それでは、最後の仕上げとして、第6章で問題形式を最終確認しましょう。本番のTOEICテストでは、この1カ月間の成果が試されるわけですが、「これだけがんばったんだから、絶対に失敗はできない」という気負いは禁物です。

　TOEICテストは、350点クリアをめざされるみなさんから、900点以上をめざす方までの英語運用能力を一度に測定します。ですから、とてもやさしい問題もあれば、むずかしい問題もあります。第1章で確認した重点パート（Part 2, Part 5, Part 7のシングルパッセージ）では2問に1問の正答が目標、それ以外のパートは3問に1問わかればOKぐらいの「リラックスした気持ち」で臨みましょう。

　こう考えて、リスニングでは、聞き逃した問題をいつまでも引きずることなく、次の問題に集中する。リーディングも、むずかしい問題はあっさり捨てて、次の問題に進む。これが実は、スピード対応能力を測定するTOEICテストで実力を発揮するコツなのです。

第6章

最終チェック

第6章の使い方

TOEIC®テストの問題形式を確認する25問の練習問題（約15分）です。第2章〜第5章でトレーニングしたあと、TOEIC®テスト受験直前に、問題形式の最終確認と準備に活用しましょう。

Part 1（写真描写問題）

写真を見ながら放送を聞いて、ABCD の英文から、写真を適切に描写しているものを選び、答えをマークします。

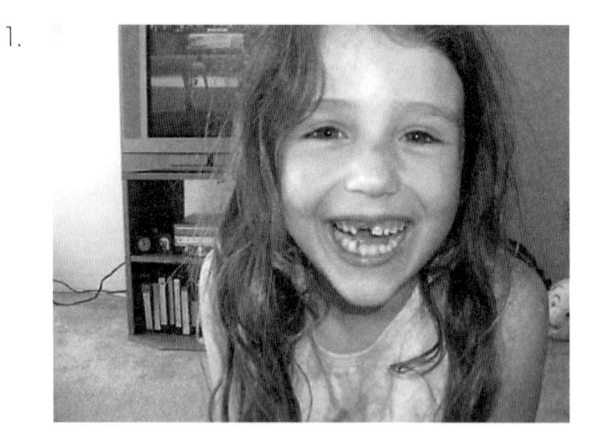

1.

Ⓐ Ⓑ Ⓒ Ⓓ

2.

Ⓐ Ⓑ Ⓒ Ⓓ

＜ワンポイント＞

Part 1 では、**人や物の状態を表わす表現**を聞き取れるかどうかが試されます。写真の人や物の状態に注意して聞きましょう。Part 1 は、**60％（10 問中 6 問）の正答**をめざしましょう。

Part 2（応答問題）

質問と、それに対する応答 ABC を聞き、解答としてふさわしいものを選び、答えをマークします。

3. Mark your answer on your answer sheet.

   Ⓐ Ⓑ Ⓒ

4. Mark your answer on your answer sheet.

   Ⓐ Ⓑ Ⓒ

5. Mark your answer on your answer sheet.

   Ⓐ Ⓑ Ⓒ

＜ワンポイント＞
Part 2 では、**問いかけの目的（情報収集、確認）**が理解できているかどうかが試されます。質問をよく聞いて理解するようにしましょう。Part 2 は、350 点突破の重点パートです。**50%（30 問中 15 問）の正答**をめざしましょう。

Part 3（会話問題）

2人の会話を聞いて、印刷された設問（3問）を解き、答えをマークします。

6. Who are the two speakers?
   (A) Athletes
   (B) A husband and wife
   (C) Coworkers
   (D) Television announcers

7. What are the two people discussing?
   (A) An announcement
   (B) A problem
   (C) A colleague
   (D) An accounting error

8. What does the conversation make clear?
   (A) The line had been shut down before.
   (B) The two speakers barely know each other.
   (C) Nothing like this has ever happened before.
   (D) Everyone simply needs to repeat what was done last time.

＜ワンポイント＞

放送が流れる前に、設問に目を通しておくと、設問の答えを探しながら聞くことができます。350点突破には、**(勘も含めて) 30％（30問中9問）の正答**で十分ですから、**最低1つだけでも目を通しておく**と余裕を持って会話を聞くことができます。なお、設問は、Who（誰が）, Where（どこで）, When（いつ）で始まるものが比較的やさしい問題です。

Part 4（説明文問題）

スピーチなどを聞いて、印刷された設問（3問）を解き、答えをマークします。

9. To whom is the person speaking?
   (A) People who have just completed a test
   (B) Job applicants
   (C) People about to take a test
   (D) Employees testing new equipment

10. Just after the announcement, what will most of the audience likely do?
    (A) Turn on their cell phones
    (B) Start reading
    (C) Hand in their booklets
    (D) Leave the room

11. What is found in front of every member of the audience?
    (A) A tray to put the booklet in
    (B) Pencils and erasers
    (C) A laptop computer
    (D) Test material

＜ワンポイント＞

Part 3 同様に、放送が流れる前に、設問に目を通しておくと、設問の答えを探しながら聞くことができます。350点突破には、**勘も含めて 30%（30問中 9問）の正答**で十分ですから、**最低 1 つだけでも目を通しておく**と、余裕を持って会話を聞くことができます。なお、設問は、Who（誰が）、Where（どこで）、When（いつ）で始まるものが比較的やさしい問題です。

Part 5（短文穴埋め問題） ＜制限時間 1 分 30 秒＞

空欄部を埋める語句を選び、センテンスを完成させ、答えをマークします。

12. The number of car accidents in the city ----- increasing in recent years.
    (A) has
    (B) are being
    (C) have been
    (D) has been

13. The government has ruled ----- any further support for the NGO because of its financial mismanagement.
    (A) off
    (B) out
    (C) in
    (D) of

14. Mark would rather ----- to the party tonight because he does not feel well.
    (A) not to go
    (B) to not go
    (C) not going
    (D) not go

＜ワンポイント＞
Part 5 では、基本的な語彙・文法を使用できるかが試されます。出題は、**単語の意味の違いを問う問題が 1/3、熟語などの慣用表現が 1/3、基本的な文法が 1/3**（主語と動詞の単数・複数の一致、時制、受動態など）です。350 点突破には、**50%（40 問中 20 問）の正答**が目標です。時間をかけすぎると、Part 7（読解問題）を解く時間が不足してしまいます。選択肢を一見して、わかりそうにない問題（単語の意味の違いなど）で時間をかけないようにしましょう。

Part 6（長文穴埋め問題） ＜制限時間 1 分 30 秒＞

3 カ所の空欄部を埋める語句を選んで文書を完成させ、答えをマークします。

Questions 15-17 refer to the following notice.

The outside lanes of Lincoln Avenue from 10th Street to 18th Street will be closed beginning Thursday, weather _____, while

15. (A) permitting
    (B) permitted
    (C) permit
    (D) permission

workers make repairs to shoulders. City officials declined to say how long the closure will remain _____. _____, work

16. (A) to effect
    (B) as an effect
    (C) effectively
    (D) in effect

17. (A) Moreover
    (B) However
    (C) Nonetheless
    (D) Particularly

on a similar stretch of Lincoln Avenue last month closed the outside lanes for three days.

＜ワンポイント＞

Part 6 では、よりライティングに近い形で、基本的な語彙・文法を正しく使用できるかどうかが試されますが、出題の内容は Part 5 とほぼ同じです。350 点突破には、**45%（12 問中 5〜6 問）の正答**が目標です。Part 5 同様に、選択肢を一見して、考えてもわかりそうにない問題（単語の意味の違いなど）は、それほど時間をかけないようにしましょう。

Part 7（読解問題－シングルパッセージ）＜制限時間3分＞

1つの英文を読んで、設問を解いて、答えをマークします。

Questions 18–20 refer to the following ad.

Bar None Children's Ranch

Kids will have the time of their lives at Bar None. Facilities include an archery range, arts and crafts center, barn and riding areas, canoeing and kayaking, hiking trails, Native American village, wall and rock climbing, zip lines and water skiing—plus so much more.

At Bar None our #1 goal is fun and participation for all. To sign up your children for any of our summer camps, just visit our Web site www.barnone.ranch.com or call 1-800-BAR-NONE (1-800-227-6663).

Bar None is located off Highway 10. Take the Trammel Exit and follow the signs.

---

18. Which of the following is included in the ad?
    (A) The history of Bar None
    (B) Estimated costs for staying at Bar None
    (C) Accounts of their experience by previous visitors to Bar None
    (D) Directions to Bar None

19. What is Bar None's chief purpose?
    (A) To let children have a good time
    (B) To teach children Native American activities
    (C) To provide children with important survival skills
    (D) To help children learn to get along well with one another

20. Who is the ad aimed at?
    (A) Children
    (B) Parents
    (C) Teenagers
    (D) Teachers

<ワンポイント>
英文を読む前に、**問題の導入文を見る**と（Questions 18–20 refer to the following **ad**.）、どんな種類の英文かがわかります。

> ad →広告（advertisement の省略）、memo →社内連絡文書（ある組織内でやり取りしている文書）、notice →お知らせ（社外など組織外の人に向けた文書）、review →批評（何かに対する評価のコメント）など。

次に、英文のタイトル（Bar None Children's Ranch）や、最初の数行（Kids will have the time of their lives at Bar None.）を読み、**何のために書かれた英文か**を把握します。続いて**設問を見て、その答えを探すように英文を読む**と、読解にかかる時間を短縮できます。なお、知らない単語の意味を考えても時間の無駄ですから、知らない単語は無視して、わかる単語から推測することが大事です。Part 7（シングルパッセージ）は、350点突破の重点パートです。**50%（28問中14問）の正答**をめざしましょう。

Part 7（読解問題－ダブルパッセージ） ＜制限時間5分＞

2つの英文を読んで、設問（5問）を解いて、答えをマークします。

Questions 21–25 refer to the following pie graph and passage.

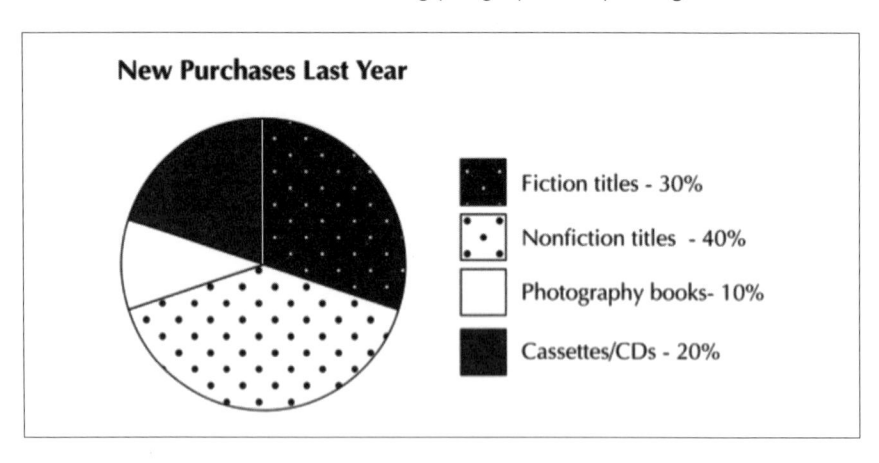

New Purchases Last Year

- Fiction titles - 30%
- Nonfiction titles - 40%
- Photography books - 10%
- Cassettes/CDs - 20%

Mr. Harold Jones, who served as chief editor of the local newspaper from 1990 to 1998, has given the city library a $10,000 donation for new purchases. Mr. Jones requires that the money be used by December 31 of this year and be spent in the following way: $1,000 for newspaper subscriptions; $4,000 for works of fiction; and $5,000 for works of nonfiction.

21. How much of its latest budget did the library spend on novels and short stories?
    (A) Almost one-third
    (B) A little over one-third
    (C) About half
    (D) The majority of its budget

22. How much more did the library spend on printed material than on audio material?
    (A) Nearly twice as much
    (B) Exactly 3 times more
    (C) Exactly 4 times more
    (D) Nearly 5 times as much

23. Which library users will benefit the least from Jones' donation?
    (A) People who check out works of fiction
    (B) People who check out CDs
    (C) People who read works of nonfiction
    (D) People who read newspapers at the library

24. What does the passage reveal about Harold Jones?
    (A) His salary
    (B) His birthplace
    (C) His current occupation
    (D) His connection to the city

25. What do the library budget and Harold Jones' donation have in common?
    (A) Most of the spending is for fiction.
    (B) Most of the spending is for nonfiction.
    (C) About the same amount is spent on newspapers.
    (D) About the same amount is spent on audio material.

＜ワンポイント＞
リーディングは全体の英文量が多いため、Part 5から順に解くと、ダブルパッセージにたどり着く頃には、十分な時間が残っていないはずです。しかし、350点突破には、**勘も含めて30％（20問中6問）の正答**で十分ですから、4セット（各5問）の中から比較的やさしそうな問題（この練習問題のように、表と文章の問題）を選んで、その問題を確実に解きましょう。

解答

Part 1

1. Look at the picture marked number 1. 1番の写真を見なさい。
   (A) The little girl is brushing her teeth.
      少女は、歯を磨いている。
   (B) The little girl has a toothache.
      少女は、歯が痛い。
   (C) The little girl has very bad teeth.
      少女には、ひどい虫歯がある。
   (D) The little girl is missing a tooth.
      少女は、歯が抜けている。

   正解：**(D)**
   解説：(A) brush one's teeth「歯磨きをする」。(B) have a toothache「歯が痛む」。(C) have bad teeth「虫歯がある」。(D) miss a tooth「歯が抜ける」。

2. Look at the picture marked number 2. 2番の写真を見なさい。
   (A) The girls are wearing uniforms.
      少女たちは、ユニフォームを着ている。
   (B) The girls are getting ready to play.
      少女たちは、試合の準備をしている。
   (C) One of the players has fallen down.
      選手の1人が転んだ。
   (D) The game has just ended.
      試合は、ちょうど終わったところだ。

   正解：**(A)**
   解説：(B) get ready to + 動詞「～する準備ができている」。(C) fall down「転ぶ」。

168

最終チェック

Part 2

3. What are we supposed to do now? 今度は何をすればいいのですか？
   (A) I don't think we are. われわれは、違うと思います。
   (B) I suppose so. そうだと思います。
   (C) That's a good question. むずかしい質問ですね。

   正解：**(C)**
   解説：「何をすべきか」を尋ねる疑問文。選択肢はいずれも疑問に対する答えは与えていないが、「むずかしい質問」と応答している (C) が正解。good question「答えの見つからない難問」。

4. Is this what you were looking for? 探していたのは、これですか？
   (A) Yes, that's me. ええ、それは私です。
   (B) Yes, where did you find it? ええ、どこで見つけました？
   (C) OK, I'll keep an eye on it. わかりました、注意しています。

   正解：**(B)**
   解説：what you were looking for「あなたが探していたもの」を尋ねる疑問文。「どこで見つけました？」と応答している (B) が正解。keep an eye on「～を注意して見ている」。

5. Shall I pick him up at the school?
   彼を学校に迎えに行きましょうか？
   (A) Thanks, please do. ありがとう、そうしてください。
   (B) Yes, I will. はい、そうします。
   (C) I think he's at school. 彼は、学校にいると思います。

   正解：**(A)**
   解説：Shall I + 動詞？は、「～しましょうか？」という申し出の表現。「そうしてください」と答えている (A) が正解。

Part 3

放送文

Questions 6–8 refer to the following conversation.

M: We need to get on top of these situations. Why are there so many delays?
W: I feel there first needs to be more accountability. There seems to be no one willing to take responsibility for the entire process.
M: I can see that. For example, last time we had the line shut down we had to go through so many channels to get it up and working again.
W: Exactly. We need one person who will be the main troubleshooter. Basically, we need someone to cut through all the red tape.

問題6–8は、次の会話に関するものです。
M: こうした事態を収拾しないといけない。なぜこれほど多くの遅れがあるのですか。
W: まずは責任をもっとはっきりさせるべきだと思います。工程全体を統括する責任者がいないようです。
M: それはわかります。たとえば、前回ラインがストップした際は、再開するためにたくさんの手続きを踏まなくてはいけなかった。
W: そのとおりです。問題解決の責任者を1人にすべきです。基本的に、形式的手続きを省く人が必要です。

語句

get on top of「(事態) を収拾する」。**delay**「遅延」。**I feel**「～と感じる」。
accountability「責任」。(**be**) **willing to** ＋**動詞**「積極的に～する」。
take responsibility for「～の責任を負う」。**process**「工程」。
I can see that. = I understand that.「それはわかります」。
we had the line shut down「われわれは、ラインをストップさせられた」。
have ＋**目的語**＋**過去分詞**で、「(物) を～される」。
go through channels「正規の手続きを踏む」。**troubleshooter**「問題を解決する人」。
cut through (**all**) **the red tape**「形式的手続きをやめにする」。

設問

6. 2人の話者は、どんな人たちですか？
   - (A) スポーツ選手
   - (B) 夫婦
   - (C) 同僚
   - (D) テレビのアナウンサー

   正解：**(C)**
   ヒント：明確に同僚だとわかる発言はないが、仕事の問題を議論している様子から推測。

7. 2人は、何について話し合っていますか？
   - (A) 案内
   - (B) 問題
   - (C) 同僚
   - (D) 経理ミス

   正解：**(B)**
   ヒント：Why are there so many delays?

8. この会話で明らかなことは、何ですか？
   - (A) 以前にラインが止まった。
   - (B) 2人の話者は、おたがいをほとんど知らない。
   - (C) こんなことはかつて起こったことがない。
   - (D) みんなが前回やったことを繰り返しさえすればいい。

   正解：**(A)**
   ヒント：last time we had the line shut down

Part 4

放送文

Questions 9–11 refer to the following instructions.
In front of you are your test booklets. This test is an open-book test. You can use / any and all of your study materials / as long as they are printed materials. This means / your text and notebooks only. No laptops can be used / during the exam. This also goes for Blackberries, as obviously Net access is not allowed / during the test. Please have the courtesy / to turn off your cell phones now. You're allowed three hours / for this test. If you finish early, please come up to the desk / and put your exam in this tray. You may now open your test booklets and begin.

問題 9–11 は、次の指示に関するものです。
（※日本語訳は、英語の原文の順序どおりに記してあります。）
みなさんの前にあるのはテスト冊子です。このテストは教科書持ち込み可です。使ってかまいません / あらゆる教材を / 印刷物である限り。つまり / 教科書とノートだけです。ラップトップを使うことはできません / 試験中に。ブラックベリーも同様です、もちろんネットへのアクセスは許されません / 試験中に。エチケットをわきまえてください / ここからは携帯電話の電源を切るという。3 時間が与えられます / このテストに。早くすんだら、デスクまで来ていただいて / テスト用紙をこのトレーに入れてください。では、テスト冊子を開いて、始めて結構です。

語句

booklet「小冊子」。open-book test「資料持ち込みが可能な試験」。any and all は、all の強調。as long as「～な限り」。laptop「ノート型パソコン」。
go for「～にあてはまる」。Blackberry「ブラックベリー（携帯情報端末）」。
obviously「明らかに」。have the courtesy to ＋ 動詞「～する礼儀をわきまえる」。
you may now begin「では、始めて結構です」。

設問

9. 話し手は、誰に話していますか？
    - (A) テストを終えたばかりの人
    - (B) 仕事の応募者
    - (C) これからテストを受ける人
    - (D) 新しい機器を試している従業員

    正解：**(C)**
    ヒント：This test is an open-book test.

10. 案内の直後、聞いていた人びとの多くは何をすると思われますか？
    - (A) 携帯電話のスイッチを入れる
    - (B) 読み始める
    - (C) 冊子を手渡す
    - (D) 部屋を出る

    正解：**(B)**
    ヒント：You may now open your test booklets and begin.

11. 話を聞いている人びと全員の前に見えるものは、何ですか？
    - (A) 冊子を入れるトレー
    - (B) 鉛筆と消しゴム
    - (C) ラップトップ・コンピュータ
    - (D) テスト用紙

    正解：**(D)**
    ヒント：In front of you are your test booklets.

Part 5

12. 市内の自動車事故の件数は、最近数年間増加している。

    正解：**(D)**
    解説：主語は、The number（単数形）。動詞が increasing（進行形）なので、has been（3人称単数形）を選ぶ。
    例文：The number of car accidents has been increasing.
    　　　自動車事故の件数は、増加している。

13. 政府は、財務の管理ミスから、そのNGOに対する引き続きの援助を禁止した。

    正解：**(B)**
    解説：文意から、慣用句 rule out「〜を禁ずる」の過去形を完成させる。further は、「それ以上の」。mismanagement は、「管理ミス」。
    例文：The government has ruled out any further support for the NGO.
    　　　政府は、そのNGOへの引き続きの援助を禁止した。

14. マークは気分がすぐれないので、今晩のパーティーに行きたくない。

    正解：**(D)**
    解説：文意から、not go を選び、慣用句 would rather + 動詞「むしろ〜したい」の否定形を完成させる。
    例文：Mark would rather not go to the party tonight.
    　　　マークは、できれば今晩のパーティーに行きたくない。

Part 6

問題 15-17 は次のお知らせに関するものです。

> 10番ストリートから18番ストリートまでのリンカーン大通りの外側（走行）車線は、天気がよければ、作業員が路肩の補修作業を行なうため、木曜日から閉鎖になります。市当局は、閉鎖がどれくらいの期間続くかについては表明を避けました。しかし、先月行なわれたリンカーン大通りの同様な区間の作業による外側（走行）車線の閉鎖は3日間でした。

15. 正解：**(A)**
    解説：文意から、weather permitting「天気がよければ」を完成させる。outside lane「外側（走行）車線」。shoulder「路肩」。
    例文：The avenue will be closed, weather permitting.
    天候がよければ、その大通りの走行車線は閉鎖になります。

16. 正解：**(D)**
    解説：文意から、in effect「（規則などが）有効な」を選ぶ。remain in effect で、「（規則が）有効な状態が続く」。
    例文：They declined to say how long the closure will remain in effect.
    彼らは、閉鎖がどれくらいの期間続くかについては表明を避けた。

17. 正解：**(B)**
    解説：文意から、However「しかしながら」を選ぶ。(A)「さらにそのうえ」、(C)「にもかかわらず」、(D)「とりわけ」。
    例文：However, work on Lincoln Avenue closed the outside lanes for three days.
    しかし、リンカーン大通りでの作業による走行車線の閉鎖は3日間でした。

Part 7（読解問題－シングルパッセージ）

問題 18–20 は次の広告に関するものです。

バー・ナン子供牧場

子供たちはバー・ナンで楽しい時間を過ごすでしょう。施設にあるのは、アーチェリー場、工芸センター、納屋と乗馬エリア、カヌーとカヤック、ハイキングコース、アメリカ原住民部落、ウォールクライミングにロッククライミング、ジップラインやウォータースキー、その他まだまだあります。

バー・ナンの第1の目的は誰もが楽しみ参加することです。われわれのサマーキャンプにお子様を参加させるためには、ホームページ www.barnone.ranch.com をご覧いただくか、1-800-BAR-NONE（1-800-227-6663）にお電話ください。

バー・ナンはハイウェイ10号を出たところにあります。トラメル出口で降りて、標識に従ってください。

語句
- **have the time of their lives**「楽しい時を過ごす」。**barn**「納屋」。
- **zip line**「傾斜を付けたワイヤーロープを、滑車にぶら下がって滑る装置」。
- **located**「～に位置している」。**off Highway 10**「ハイウェイ10号を降りたところ」。

18. 広告に含まれているのは、次のどれですか？
    (A) バー・ナンの歴史
    (B) バー・ナンでの宿泊の費用見積もり
    (C) 以前にバー・ナンを訪れた人びとの報告
    (D) バー・ナンへの道案内

    正解：**(D)**
    ヒント：Bar None is located off Highway 10. Take the Trammel Exit and follow the signs.

19. バー・ナンの主たる目的は、何ですか？
    (A) 子供たちに楽しい時を過ごさせる
    (B) 子供たちにアメリカ原住民の活動を教える
    (C) 子供たちに大切なサバイバル術を教える
    (D) 子供たちが上手な人付き合いを学ぶ手助けをする

    正解：**(A)**
    ヒント：At Bar None our #1 goal is fun and participation for all.

20. この広告の対象は、誰ですか？
    (A) 子供たち
    (B) 保護者
    (C) ティーンエイジャーたち
    (D) 先生たち

    正解：**(B)**
    ヒント：To sign up your children for any of our summer camps

Part 7（読解問題ーダブルパッセージ）

問題 21–25 は、次のグラフと文書に関するものです。

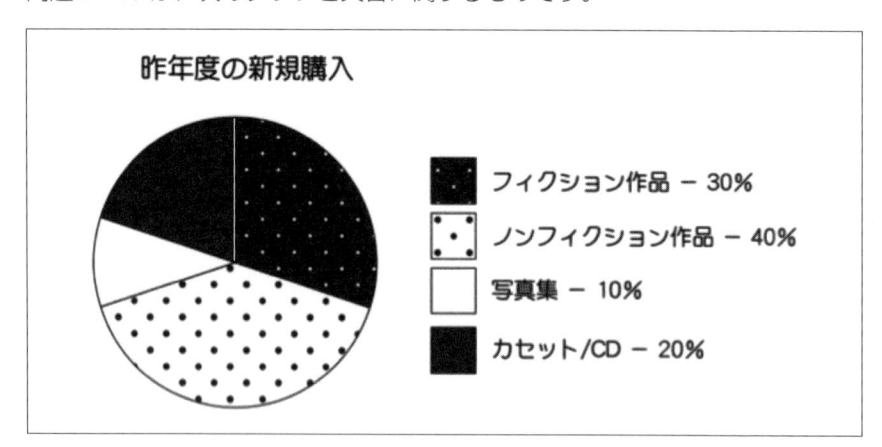

```
昨年度の新規購入

■ フィクション作品 － 30%
・ ノンフィクション作品 － 40%
□ 写真集 － 10%
■ カセット/CD － 20%
```

ハロルド・ジョーンズ氏は、1990 年から 1998 年まで地元新聞の編集長として勤務し、新規購入のために、市立図書館に 1 万ドルの寄付をしています。ジョーンズ氏は、そのお金を今年の 12 月 31 日までに、以下の要領で使うよう求めています。新聞の購読に 1,000 ドル、フィクション作品に 4,000 ドル、ノンフィクション作品に 5,000 ドル。

語句
fiction「小説」。nonfiction「ノンフィクション（伝記、歴史などの作品）」。
chief editor「編集長」。donation「寄付」。in the following way「以下の方法で」。
subscription「定期購読」。

21. 図書館は、最近の予算のうちどれくらいを小説と短編小説に使っていますか？
    (A) ほぼ3分の1
    (B) 3分の1よりやや多め
    (C) およそ半分
    (D) 予算の大部分

    正答：**(A)**
    ヒント：上段の図の Fiction titles – 30%

22. 図書館は、音声製品よりどれくらい多く印刷物に予算を使っていますか？
    (A) ほぼ2倍多く
    (B) ちょうど3倍多く
    (C) ちょうど4倍多く
    (D) ほぼ5倍多く

    正答：**(C)**
    ヒント：上段の図の Cassettes/CDs-20%、他の印刷物は 80%

23. ジョーンズの寄付の恩恵がもっとも少ない図書館利用者は、誰ですか？
    (A) フィクションの作品を借りる人びと
    (B) CDを借りる人びと
    (C) ノンフィクションの作品を読む人びと
    (D) 図書館で新聞を読む人びと

    正答：**(B)**
    ヒント：下段の文の $1,000 for newspaper subscriptions; $4,000 for works of fiction; and $5,000 for works of nonfiction.

24. ハロルド・ジョーンズについてこの文書から明らかなことは、何ですか？
    - (A) 彼の給料
    - (B) 彼の生誕地
    - (C) 彼の現在の職業
    - (D) 彼の市との関係

    正答：**(D)**

    ヒント：下段の文の Mr. Harold Jones, who served as chief editor of the local newspaper from 1990 to 1998, has given the city library a $10,000 donation for new purchases.

25. 図書館の予算とハロルド・ジョーンズの寄付に共通なことは、何ですか？
    - (A) ほとんどの支出がフィクション用である。
    - (B) ほとんどの支出がノンフィクション用である。
    - (C) ほぼ同額が新聞に使われている。
    - (D) ほぼ同額が音声製品に使われている。

    正答：**(B)**

    ヒント：上段の図の Nonfiction titles-40% と、下段の文章の $1,000 for newspaper subscriptions; $4,000 for works of fiction; and $5,000 for works of nonfiction.

＜ワンポイント＞

ダブルパッセージの問題は、2つの英文を読んで、5つの設問に答えることが求められます。でも、焦る必要はありません。前述のとおり、350点突破には、**勘も含めて30％（20問中6問）の正答**で十分です。4セット（各5問）の中から比較的やさしそうな問題をまずチェックして、各英文の最初の数行を読み、**それぞれは何のために書かれた英文か**を把握します。これで、設問を読んだ際に、**どちらの英文から答えを探すように読めばよいのか**がわかります。比較的やさしい問題であれば、5分で1セット（5問）が解けます。最後まで、あきらめずにがんばりましょう！

本書の第2章〜第5章は、学習者向け英字新聞『週刊ST』(ジャパンタイムズ) に、2002年4月〜2010年3月までの8年間 (400回) にわたって掲載された「TOEIC® テスト 実践トレーニング」の練習問題に加筆したものです。

●編集協力
　杉山まどか

●社内協力
　高見沢紀子・菅田晶子・小倉宏子・吉井瑠里・宮内繭子

●CD製作協力
　Peter Serafin and Xanthe Smith(Golden Angel Studio)[「語句」「指示文」ほかナレーション]
　吉田美穂(俳協)[「語句」日本語ナレーション]
　佐藤京子(東京録音)

●著者紹介

http://www.icconsul.com/

鹿野　晴夫（かの　はるお）

　1964年北海道生まれ。東京都立大学工学部卒。現在、英語トレーニングのICC東京本校責任者。英語レベル別指導法のエキスパートとして、企業・大学で「英語トレーニング法」の講演・セミナーを多数担当するほか、英語教員向けに「英語トレーニングの指導法セミナー」を担当している。著書に、自らの学習経験を綴った「TOEIC®テスト 300点から800点になる学習法」「TOEIC®テスト 900点を突破する集中トレーニング」（以上、中経出版）をはじめとするTOEIC®テスト関連の著作が40点以上。2010年には、『TOEIC®テスト　スピーキング／ライティング問題集』（研究社、千田潤一と共著）も刊行。

TOEIC®テスト　これだけ　直前1カ月　350点クリア

初版発行	2011年4月28日	
著者	鹿野晴夫	
	Copyright © 2011 by ICC	
発行者	関戸雅男	KENKYUSHA
発行	株式会社　研究社	〈検印省略〉
	〒102-8152　東京都千代田区富士見2-11-3	
	電話　営業 03(3288)7777(代)　編集 03(3288)7711(代)	
	振替　00150-9-26710	
	http://www.kenkyusha.co.jp	
印刷所	研究社印刷株式会社	

＊

装丁・CDデザイン	久保和正
本文レイアウト・組版	(株)インフォルム
CD編集・製作	(株)東京録音

ISBN978-4-327-43069-6 C1082

本書の全部または一部を無断で複写複製（コピー）することは、著作権法上での例外を除き禁じられています。
価格はカバーに表示してあります。

研究社の出版案内

直前1カ月は、これだけきっちり仕上げよう！

鹿野晴夫〔著〕

TOEIC® テスト これだけ 直前1カ月 470点クリア

英語力をのばしたい！
1カ月で確実にTOEIC®のスコアがアップ！

A5判 並製 184頁
ISBN 978-4-327-43070-2 C1082

CD付き

TOEIC® テスト これだけ 直前1カ月 600点クリア

TOEIC® テスト直前1カ月で、さらにスコアアップをはかりたい！

A5判 並製 184頁
ISBN 978-4-327-43071-9 C1082

CD付き

▶ TOEIC®テストのスコアを上げたい。
▶ でも、あまり時間がない。
▶ 通勤・通学の時間を有効に使いたい。

そんなみなさんのために、TOEIC®の問題形式に慣れるだけでなく、基本的な英語力のアップがはかれるように工夫しました。
『週刊ST』の人気コラムに大幅加筆して単行本化！

出版社による初のTOEIC® SWテスト実戦問題集！

TOEIC® テスト スピーキング／ライティング問題集

千田潤一・鹿野晴夫〔著〕

A5判 並製 180頁
ISBN 978-4-327-43068-9 C1082

CD付き